MAKING THE NET WORK

SUSTAINABLE DEVELOPMENT
IN A DIGITAL SOCIETY

RSA

The Royal Society for the encouragement
of Arts, Manufactures & Commerce

Founded in 1754

RSA Library
8 John Adam Street London WC2N 6EZ
+44 (0)20 7451 6874
library@rsa.org.uk
www.theRSA.org

Digital Europe

Research partners

Forum for the **Future**

**Science Centre
North Rhine-Westphalia**
Institute of Work
and Technology

Institute for Culture
Studies
Wuppertal Institute for
**Climate, Environment and
Energy**

Corporate and regional partners

Cymru Ar-lein
Online for a Better Wales

**Cynulliad Cenedlaethol Cymru
The National Assembly for Wales**

in vent

Supported by the European Commission

Information Society
Technologies

MAKING THE NET WORK

SUSTAINABLE DEVELOPMENT IN A DIGITAL SOCIETY

Written by Vidhya Alakeson
Tim Aldrich, James Goodman and
Britt Jorgensen

Forewords by Jonathon Porritt and
Erkki Liikanen

This edition first published by Xeris Publishing Company

Xeris Publishing Company Limited
78 Waldegrave Road
Teddington
Middlesex TW11 8NY
England

British Library Cataloguing in Publication Data
Data available

Library of Congress in Publication Data
A catalogue record has been applied for

1 3 5 7 9 10 8 6 4 2

ISBN 0-9546216-0-3

Typeset by Regent Typesetting, London
Printed by Bell and Bain Ltd., Glasgow

CONTENTS

LIST OF FIGURES

LIST OF TEXT BOXES

ABOUT THE AUTHORS

Vidhya Alakeson, **Tim Aldrich**, **James Goodman** and **Britt Jorgensen** are all researchers at Forum for the Future where they specialize in the relationship between technology and sustainable development.

Forum for the Future is a UK-based sustainable development charity working to accelerate the transition to a sustainable way of life. It develops partnerships with business, local authorities, regional bodies and universities and seeks to influence a wider network of decision makers and opinion formers through cutting edge projects. www.forumforthefuture.org.uk

About the contributors

Ian Christie is an associate of the UK-based think tank New Economics Foundation and www.opendemocracy.net

Diane Coyle runs the consultancy Enlightenment Economics, is a member of the UK Competition Commission and the author of best-selling books including *Sex, Drugs and Economics*, *Paradoxes of Prosperity* and *The Weightless World*.

Sean Gilbert is senior associate at the Global Reporting Initiative, and has extensive international experience in sustainability reporting, performance metrics and development of standardized reporting frameworks.

Peter James is co-director of SustainIT, an initiative of the research centre UK CEED. He is also visiting professor of environmental management at Bradford University.

Kate Oakley is an associate director of the Local Futures Group and an associate of the think tank Demos, as well as being a writer and consultant on issues concerning new technologies and entrepreneurship.

Richard Reeves is a writer, speaker and consultant. He regularly contributes to *Management Today*, the *Observer*, *New Statesman*, the *Guardian* and other publications. His latest book is *Happy Mondays–Putting The Pleasure Back Into Work*.

Paul Resnick is associate professor at the University of Michigan School of Information, and has previously worked with AT&T Labs and at MIT. His research focuses on sociotechnical capital and recommender systems.

Friedrich Schmidt-Bleek is the inventor of the Factor X and MIPS concept. He is the president of the Factor 10 Institute and the Factor 10 Club and the author of best-selling books including *The Fossil Makers* and *MIPS Konkret*.

David Weinberger is co-author of the legendary book *The Cluetrain Manifesto*. He is now editor of the *Journal of the Hyperlinked Organization*, writes for magazines and newspapers including *Wired* and *The New York Times*, as well as working as an independent strategic marketing consultant.

ACKNOWLEDGEMENTS

This book wouldn't have been possible without the research, advice and expertise of colleagues at the Wuppertal Institute and the Fondazione Eni Enrico Mattei (FEEM) who worked with us on the Digital Europe project. Our thanks go to Justus von Geibler, Michael Kuhndt, Stephan Moll, Michael Ritthoff, Karl Otto Schallaböck, Sören Steger, Volker Türk and Iris Utzmann at the Wuppertal Institute, and Elena Bellini, Martina Gambaro, Carole Maignan, Gianmarco Ottaviano and Dino Pinelli at FEEM.

The support and cooperation of the project's partners in business and regional government has been invaluable. Special thanks to Katrina Giles at AOL Europe; Phil Case at Barclays; Kate Dunning at EMI; Chris Tuppen and Ama Dadson at GeSI; Zoe McMahon and Jonathan Wood at HP; Charlotte Grezo and Nick Hughes at Vodafone; and Diana Reynolds at the Welsh Assembly Government, for their help and commitment to the project. Thanks also to Heidi Seybert and Peter Johnston in the Information Society Directorate General of the European Commission for their assistance and support.

We'd like to thank Paul Miller and James Wilsdon at Demos for their invaluable contribution to Digital Europe during their time at Forum for the Future.

Thanks also to Ian Christie, Diane Coyle, Sean Gilbert, Peter James, Erkki Liikanen, Kate Oakley, Jonathon Porritt, Richard Reeves, Paul Resnick, Frederick Schmidt-Bleek and David Weinberger for their contributions to the book.

During the writing of this book, many people have commented on drafts and offered knowledge and insight. We're grateful to Elena Bonfiglioli, Edward Brewster, Nevin Cohen, Judith Doyle, Gilles Duranton, Andy Gillespie, Peter Hesseldal, Lorenz Hilty, Peter Maxson, Justine Parkinson, Christian Seelos, Bill Thompson and Will Davies.

Thanks to Lisa Greaves for expert proofreading and Neil Morgan and Paula Snell for graphs and logos. Thanks also to Caroline Broughton and Noel McPherson at Xeris.

Finally, thanks to everyone at Forum for the Future.

FOREWORD

by Jonathon Porritt, Programme Director of Forum for the Future and Chair of the UK Sustainable Development Commission

Coverage of IT issues in the media has changed dramatically over the last couple of years. Gone are the stories of how ecommerce is retuning the engines of the economy, or how the Internet and ebusiness herald a new age of limitless growth and productivity gains. The long-awaited battalions of click-happy consumers seem to be lying low, still hesitant and only half-committed to the new ways of shopping or doing business. These days, it's much more common to read about the exploits of text-messaging teenagers, or how the Internet is being used to organize mass public protest. Stories of the new economy have been replaced by stories of the emerging new society.

Of course, ecommerce is still very much with us and the debate over the new economy in the business press and universities rages on; it's just that the headlines have changed. This may be down to the whimsy of the modern media machine, but it could also be a reflection of where the enduring value of information and communication technology (ICT) lies.

From Stephenson's steam locomotive to the mobile phone, technological development has powerfully shaped our shared notions of progress. New technology has played an increasingly important role in driving economic growth, stimulating new markets and ever-higher levels of consumer demand. New technologies have played an equally crucial part in the contemporary debate about sustainable development. For many, it is the sheer momentum of technology-driven progress that poses the greatest threat to the integrity of the natural world, with each new misguided technological development leading to new levels of unsustainable growth, eating up resources on an unprecedented scale, and making the prospects of a healthy and prosperous life for future generations a shade bleaker than they already were.

ICT clearly shares many of the downsides of technology in general, as the research presented in this book amply demonstrates. The manufacture of hardware requires large quantities of raw materials and energy. Even products that appear to be 'virtual', such as digital music files or banking transactions made over the Internet, have physical impacts that exist in the real world. It is dangerous and unhelpful to suggest, as some have done, that today's 'knowledge economy' is automatically and in all circumstances less demanding of our precious natural resources.

What's more, it's impossible not to be alarmed by some of the more pernicious effects of modern ICT use. The anonymity of the Internet provides the perfect cloak for child pornographers. And the use of more and more ICT by more and more people seems to be having a deleterious effect on our ability to control the speed of life, with the result that people now feel more highly stressed and less satisfied with their working lives, as statistics show.

But even so, there is a tantalizing suggestion that ICT brings an exciting new ingredient to the traditional formuli of economic growth and progress. The argument of this book is less about how ICT has an impact on existing behaviour – as if society and technology somehow developed in isolation and were then suddenly brought together – and more about how ICT is helping to reconfigure the relationships between people and organizations in more fundamental ways – ways that put the human species in a better position to face the challenge of sustainable development. To take just one example, there is no doubt in my mind that global problems like climate change and poverty require solutions on a global scale, and ICT is certainly joining people up across borders, as they have never been joined up before.

What I particularly like is that here we have a book about the relationship between ICT and sustainable development that reminds us of the importance of shared social values in creating any sort of change. If 'making the net work' means using ICT to realign our values to those of sustainable development, then we're talking about technological progress of a very different kind.

FOREWORD

by Erkki Liikanen, European Commissioner for Enterprise and the Information Society

Sustainable development implies integrating economic, social and environmental issues. It should not be seen as a limitation to growth and employment, but rather as an attractive enabler for investment, prosperity, welfare and social justice. The knowledge-based economy is critical for this kind of sustainable growth.

The promotion of a sustainable knowledge economy has been high on the EU policy agenda since the Lisbon and Gothenburg European Councils in March 2000 and June 2001. The Lisbon strategy focuses on making Europe the most competitive and dynamic knowledge-based economy in the world, capable of sustainable economic growth with more and better jobs and greater social cohesion. The strategy agreed at the Gothenburg Council made particular reference to the environmental dimension of sustainability and the need to develop new technologies that use fewer resources and reduce pollution.

Information and communication technology (ICT) can create major opportunities, not only for growth and competitiveness, but also for employment, social cohesion and the environment, contributing to sustainable development.

Broadband Internet access provides the backbone for the Information Society and should contribute directly to greater economic and social cohesion in Europe. The networked economy is transforming our society and, in the coming decades, social changes are likely to be more extensive and to happen much faster than at any time in the past, because the technologies driving them are continuing to develop at an ever increasing pace.

Grid technologies – linking many computers up to perform common tasks – will have a profound and unprecedented effect on almost every aspect of our lives: private, social, cultural, economic or political. Grids are creating a

European information and communications infrastructure that reinforces the transition towards an inclusive knowledge based information society.

However, these benefits will not be delivered unless the supporting policies, frameworks and measures are put in place to address them. We should continue to strive to achieve not only access to the web for all Europe's citizens, enterprises and governments, but also to bring the knowledge and networks that the web enables within easy reach.

There are still noteworthy differences between sectors and regions, and companies are facing the challenge of adopting more advanced solutions to improve productivity. In many respects, we are still in a transition period, experiencing growing pains and learning through experience.

New business models for connecting businesses with their partners and suppliers over the Internet are being developed. Key sources of competitive advantage no longer lie in low-cost manufacturing, but in the adoption and synthesis of technological, organizational and managerial innovations to enhance productivity. In addition, given the goals of sustainable growth, there is certainly a need for a more balanced integration of economic, social and environmental concerns into business strategies.

Since its launch in July 2001, the Digital Europe project has made critical progress in identifying synergies between ebusiness and sustainable development and addressing further challenges for promoting a sustainable knowledge economy. It has studied a variety of relevant issues such as the dematerialization of products and services, resource and transport efficiency improvements, the integration of social and environmental considerations into ebusiness models and corporate social responsibility, as well as factors enhancing competitiveness and quality of life in the regions.

Making the Net Work contributes to a better understanding of the environmental, social and regional impacts of ICT. It also makes a valuable contribution to future debates on how to decouple economic growth from resource use and foster digital inclusion. It provides new insights on how the relevant decision makers in private and public organizations could refine their operations and policies to enable sustainable development to become a reality.

INTRODUCTION

What do PlayStation 2 and an endangered species of gorilla have in common? The answer is a hard, grey, acid-resistant metal called tantalum, found in abundance in the Democratic Republic of Congo.

Most of the world's tantalum is used by the electronics industry. It's the metal in capacitors that makes the miniaturization of electronic products possible. In 2000, a few months before the launch of PlayStation 2 and in the heat of the consumer boom in mobile phones, the price of tantalum rocketed, due to a combination of unprecedented demand, overzealous forecasts and market speculation. The results were devastating for the Kahuzi-Biega national park, where much of the Congo's tantalum deposits are found. It's a world heritage site and home to 86 per cent of the world's population of the eastern lowlands gorilla, also known as Grauer's gorilla.

With tantalum suddenly so lucrative, as many as 10,000 people moved into the tantalum mines. Farmers abandoned their fields and were joined by professional miners, Rwandan prisoners of war and thousands of young men and children forced into labour by the local militia who control the mines. They brought with them 300 bushmeat hunters armed with Kalashnikov rifles to go out and hunt for food in the rainforest.

It's estimated that all of the park's 3,700 elephants were killed, and the population of Grauer's gorilla fell from 17,000 to under 3,000. By March 2001 the miners had to subsist on tortoises, birds and small mammals. Hunting trips had previously taken only a day. Now they were lasting a week and hunters often came back empty-handed.

As this bizarre and tragic story reminds us, actions can have unpredictable outcomes: market speculation on the price of an obscure metal can endanger wildlife in the Congo. What appeared initially to be an economic problem of managing supply and demand had social and environmental consequences of a severity that took the electronics industry by surprise.

Recognition of the interconnections between human and natural systems lies at the heart of sustainable development. Sustainable development attempts to integrate social, environmental and economic dimensions in order to build a world that is safer, more equitable and uses natural systems in a way that protects them for future generations. According to Jonathon Porritt: 'sustainable development is the only game in town which stands a chance of delivering the scale of change necessary to meet our present and future needs and responsibilities'.

The goal of creating a more sustainable world is a real and pressing one. At a glance, any number of indicators tells us that we're heading in the wrong direction:

- 40 to 50 per cent of the population of sub-Saharan Africa goes hungry every day and the region is worse off nutritionally in 2003 than it was 30 years ago.
- Over 100 million Europeans and North Americans live in cities where the air is unsafe to breathe.
- If we carry on burning fossil fuels at present rates greenhouse gases in the atmosphere will increase by 50 per cent within 15 years, risking catastrophic climate shifts.
- 12 per cent of bird species, 25 per cent of mammal species and 34 per cent of fish species are under threat of extinction.
- Global consumption of minerals, wood, plastic and other materials increased by 240 per cent between 1960 and 1995.

Each of these trends is worrying in itself; but together they present us with an enormous and complex challenge. This book is about the role that information and communication technology (ICT), in particular the Internet and the mobile telephone, has in providing desperately needed solutions.

The Internet is the biggest shared space for communication that has ever existed, and anyone (with the right means) is welcome to participate. It hosts the biggest library that has ever existed and it's available for anyone (with the right means) to browse its corridors and aisles. It's the 'net' in the title of this book; and with the mobile telephone, we have another net, a moving, changing net of possible links between people, that is also beginning to be tied to the Internet.

Much of the trading that set off the tantalum boom took place on the Internet, a medium that allows instantaneous transactions. The same medium meant that news of the destruction of the Kahuzi-Biega national park could spread further and quicker than would have been possible before.

These two ICTs are helping to change the way that humans communicate, widening the possibilities on a scale that is both fantastic and frightening. They're transforming the way we live and work, our social relationships and communities, even our impact on the environment.

The growth of ICT shouldn't be seen in isolation. It's part of a long-term shift away from the industrial economy, based on the production of manufactured goods, towards an economy focused on the delivery of services. Over the course of the twentieth century, service sector employment in France rose steadily from 25 per cent in 1900 to 70 per cent in 1990.[1] The shift has gathered momentum in recent years, spurred on by two complementary trends. One is the uptake of ICT. The other is the emergence of knowledge as the driver of economic success. Between 1992 and 1999, knowledge intensive employment (scientists, engineers, ICT specialists and so on) grew faster than all other types of employment across OECD countries.[2] The knowledge-driven economy and the high-tech economy go hand in hand, each reinforcing the other.

Because of these structural changes, the potential for transformation in the societies we live in and the economies that serve us has increased. But can we realize this potential and make ICT work for sustainable development? This book argues that we *can* – and we're not alone in believing this. The Welsh Assembly Government in the UK is one of only a small number of legislative bodies that uses sustainable development as an organizing principle across all departments and its policies on ICT are designed with this in mind. As Erikki Liikanen mentions in his Foreword, policy makers in the European Union are explicit about using ICT to transform Europe into the most dynamic – and sustainable – knowledge economy in the world. The Millennium Development Goals, agreed at the UN's Millennium Summit in 2000, aim to 'integrate the principles of sustainable development into country policies and programmes' and to 'make available the benefits of new technologies – especially information and communications technologies'. Few would claim that sustainable development has yet made the impact it needs to at the level necessary to create real change. But the idea that ICT and the knowledge economy could be a win-win opportunity for growth, social cohesion and the environment is creeping in at the margins and – we hope – growing in strength and credibility.

Making the Net Work is the culmination of a pan-European research project funded by the European Commission to investigate the link between ICT and sustainable development. The project, called 'Digital Europe', followed hot on the heels of the publication of *Digital Futures: Living in a Dot-com World*, also produced by Forum for the Future. Like a number of other projects, books and papers, *Digital Futures* argued that the new technologies could be important for sustainable development. It came at a time when the overwhelming majority of attention was directed at the economic opportunities of ICT in the narrowest sense, and set out an agenda for change that is still very relevant. Fast, cheap global communications could reduce the need for travel, so pollution levels would fall. Online communities could provide much needed social support in the absence of strong local ties. Access to global knowledge networks could create new economic opportunities away from cities, giving rural areas a much needed boost.

Building on these early ideas, Digital Europe set out to understand more about how ICT is produced and used, generate data on its social and environmental impacts and provide ideas on how the technology could best serve the interests of everyone.

The project was set up in July 2001 and from the outset involved a broad consortium of interested parties, including regional bodies and a number of companies in the ICT sector or using ICT in a fundamental area of their business [see Box 1.1]. Leading the research were teams from Forum for the Future in the UK, the Wuppertal Institute in Germany and the Fondazione Eni Enrico Mattei (FEEM) in Italy.

The research involved a range of case studies focusing on areas of particular interest, such as the social and environmental role of ebanking or the environmental impacts of mobile computing. This partnership approach to the research gave us access to information on trends and strategies that otherwise would have been difficult to find. It also provided us with insights into corporate policy-making, in particular where corporate social responsibility (CSR) – the business response to sustainable development – was concerned. Many of the ideas and solutions you'll read about in this book have been developed together with our partners, taking account of the need for companies to align their CSR programmes with core business goals.

The Digital Europe project team also commissioned a survey of European businesses to find out how they were using ICT to help manage their social and environmental impacts. And we conducted a wide range of interviews with leading thinkers and practitioners in the area. Much of this information is collected on a project website, where the research reports can be downloaded for free.[3]

Digital Europe focused on the role of business in making the digital society more sustainable and this is reflected in *Making the Net Work*. Historically, business has been at the heart of social change. When Henry Ford started the mass production of combustion engine cars in the early 1900s in the USA, he did more than create a convenient, affordable form of transport for the middle classes; he changed the social life of America's cities. With people far less restricted in how far they could travel, they were able to escape the city for a better quality of life. What emerged was American suburbia.

Our interest in the role of business recognizes the pivotal role that it has today. As the major wealth generator in society, any attempt to create a more sustainable future depends on getting business on board. A shift in business

Box 1.1 *Digital Europe partners*

AOL Europe
Barclays
EMI
Global eSustainability Initiative (GeSI)
Hewlett Packard (HP)
Sun Microsystems
Vodafone Group

Regional government was represented by the Ruhr region in Germany
and the Welsh Assembly Government in the UK.

attitudes towards more sustainable development could be the spur needed to
shift the entire system. But we don't focus exclusively on business. Delivering
more sustainable development depends on the involvement of all sectors of
society, including governments, consumers and citizens. Ultimately, the book
is intended for anyone with an interest in sustainable development, new technology, or both.

Each of the three research partners involved in Digital Europe researched a
different area of impact. FEEM investigated the relationship between the use
of ICT and regional economies in Europe. The Wuppertal Institute led with
research on the material intensity of ICT and its potential to contribute to
'dematerialization' – a relative reduction in resource use – in the European
economy. Forum for the Future concentrated on the social role of ICT, focusing in particular on the response of business to the opportunities for greater
social responsibility.

The various findings from these three research strands are all built into the
pages of *Making the Net Work*. But the process of writing this book, integrating
two years of research, has introduced a new question to add to the one we set
out with. We started the project asking: 'What effect does the use of ICT have
on society and the environment?' but trying to answer this has led us to add
the question: 'How is ICT affecting our ability to cope with the challenge of
sustainable development?'. Our contention is that, as ICT becomes more
sophisticated and more embedded in our organizational structures and everyday life, we are in a better position than ever before to make sustainable development work.

Of course, this is not an automatic process that we can now sit back and
watch, content in the knowledge that ICT is going to save the world. The

lesson of looking at a new, massively enabling technology like ICT reaffirms the fact that there are no easy solutions to the challenges that we face. What we really need is commitment, concerted action and radical change. Therefore, *Making the Net Work* puts forward plenty of practical recommendations for business, government, consumers and citizens. Perhaps the clearest message that we hope you will take away with you after having read this book is that values matter. The values of those who design, market, implement and use ICT is really what will decide whether or not the technology will work for sustainable development. In the digital society, values are more powerful than ever. Aligning the values of the digital society to sustainable development is what will make the real difference.

Each chapter of the book builds on preceding chapters, but depending on which aspects of the digital society you're most interested in, you might want to turn to a particular chapter.

If you want to find out more about the networks that underpin our complex world and explore how a more connected world could be a more sustainable one, then take a look at 'Netting The Globe'.

If you want to find out how unprecedented access to information through ICT can empower individuals in the interests of sustainable development, 'Infoworld' offers some insights.

If you're interested in how ICT can help rebuild trust in society and why trust is important for sustainable development, turn to 'Webs Of Trust'.

If you're curious about virtualization and how it could improve the environmental impacts of products and services, you'll find new data and analysis in 'Virtually Sustainable'.

If you're concerned about how technology is speeding up society and want a fresh take on the consequences for sustainable development, then take a look at 'Faster Is Different'.

We've also included contributions from a number of respected writers and researchers in the field of ICT and sustainable development. You can hear from:

- writer David Weinberger about the new worlds created by ICT;
- economist Diane Coyle on measuring the contribution of ICT to growth and productivity;
- Ian Christie on the importance of cultivating empathy for sustainable development;
- Kate Oakley of the Local Futures Group on a new vision for the knowledge-based economy;
- Friedrich Schmidt-Bleek of the Factor 10 Institute on the prospects for ICT and resource efficiency;

- Peter James of the UK Centre for Economic and Environmental Development (UKCEED) on 'smart services';
- Paul Resnick of the University of Michigan on social capital in the digital society;
- Sean Gilbert of the Global Reporting Initiative on sustainability reporting in the ICT sector; and
- Richard Reeves on the need for social innovation to match technological change in the workplace.

Before we dive in to explore these different aspects of the digital society, we'll take a look in the first chapter at some of the economy-wide evidence we collected during Digital Europe. Is the use of ICT leading to greater resource efficiency? Can we see the signs of a more inclusive regional economy? Is there, in short, a more sustainable economic paradigm waiting just round the corner?

SUSTAINABLE DEVELOPMENT IN
THE DIGITAL SOCIETY

Digitopia's favourite visionary Nicholas Negroponte wrote: 'Granted, if you make pizzas you need to be close to the dough; if you're a surgeon you must be close to your patients (at least for the next two decades). But if your trade involves bits (not atoms), you probably don't need to be anywhere specific – at least most of the time.'[1] Negroponte was suggesting something quite radical: that ICT was going to fundamentally remake the way that humans have interacted with each other and their environment. The ability to transfer information virtually, at high speed and almost no cost, and to communicate effectively at a distance would allow companies to locate away from established economic hubs, free workers to work from anywhere and, in doing so, reduce the environmental impact of goods and people moving from place to place. It was on the basis of this kind of vision that many of the hopes for a new paradigm of sustainability rested.

We embarked on the Digital Europe project in search of evidence of this new paradigm taking shape at the economy-wide level. We chose to concentrate on areas where the sustainability potential of ICT had prompted particular excitement, hoping to clarify the real opportunities for positive change through our research. The following made the short list:

- the possibility of distributing economic opportunities more evenly across and between regions;
- the ability to work effectively away from the office; and
- the prospect of breaking the link between economic growth and resource use.

In this chapter, we'll take you through the findings of our research in these three areas. In each case, we'll explore how the issue in question fits within the context of sustainable development. Then we'll look at the assumptions underpinning early optimism that ICT would promote change in the interests of sustainable development. And finally, we'll examine the evidence as to whether or not this is happening.

You'll see that a relatively mixed picture emerges in which the effects of ICT are ambivalent: it is neither undermining attempts to create a more sustainable future, nor actively promoting more sustainable development.

Reshaping Europe's landscape

In nineteenth-century America there were as many as 250 stock exchanges serving predominantly local markets. With the introduction of the telegraph, almost overnight the New York Stock Exchange was transformed from a local to a national exchange. The exchange in Hartford, Connecticut survived until 1933, but within two years of a direct long distance telephone line to New York being laid, it closed. The arrival of the telegraph and telephone in America reduced communications costs and in time the entire economic landscape of the country was transformed. By reducing the significance of distance, technology can change our relationship with place. But why does this matter for sustainable development?

A sustainable society should provide individuals with, among other things, access to varied and satisfying opportunities for work, personal creativity and recreation. If all individuals are to enjoy access to such benefits, economic activity needs to be evenly distributed across regions. This doesn't mean that it should be evenly dispersed down to the last village or hamlet. Entirely dispersed activity is neither realistic, nor necessarily desirable. People and firms engaged in the same kind of activity will frequently gather together to gain access to critical resources, share knowledge and improve efficiency. For example, just as medieval scholars gathered in Bologna and Paris to share intellectual resources, industrialists transformed the Ruhr Valley and northern Italy into Europe's manufacturing powerhouses, taking advantage of natural resources, labour markets and conducive business environments. What's more, entirely dispersed activity can be environmentally inefficient, for instance, increasing the distance that people and goods have to travel. In the interests of sustainable development, we should look to promote a more even distribution of economic clusters across regions.

But this isn't the picture we see in Europe today. Strong imbalances in economic development persist between Europe's regions. The richest region of Europe is central London, with a gross domestic product (GDP) per head 2.7 times the average for EU member and accession states (EU25). That's 9 times higher than the poorest region, Lubelskie in eastern Poland, with a GDP per head of less than a third of the EU25 average.[2] Plotting Europe's richest regions on a map, a distinct core periphery pattern emerges, with Europe's wealthy regions forming a core that runs from London down through to northern Italy.

Could today's ICT reshape Europe's economic landscape, breaking this pattern and encouraging clusters to develop elsewhere, creating several economic hubs across Europe? Or would it have a similar effect to the telegraph, promoting centralization and the dominance of the European core?

The forces that cause industries to cluster or disperse are called centripetal and centrifugal forces. Centripetal forces promote clustering and centrifugal forces encourage dispersion. One of the main reasons why firms cluster is the need to share knowledge and information about changes in the market, innovations and so on. Where firms cluster, all benefit from the flow of relevant information and knowledge. ICT makes it possible to share this, no matter what the distance. Data can be transferred across the globe in seconds at almost no cost.

Initially, there seemed every reason to assume that ICT would weaken centripetal forces, allowing industries to set up away from the core without increasing their costs or reducing their ability to benefit from knowledge sharing. These assumptions were quickly challenged by the emergence of Silicon Valley in California as the motor of the high-tech revolution, suggesting that ICT was not weakening centripetal forces after all. In short, the signals were mixed about whether ICT was going to create more balanced spatial development in Europe.

As part of Digital Europe, researchers from FEEM set out to gain a clearer understanding of the impact of ICT on clustering in specific industries. They measured change in the location of different industries between 1980 and 2000, firstly across the 15 member states of the EU and then across Italy's 103 provinces. If an industry grows faster in a location where it is already over-represented, this is a sign of its tendency to cluster. By selecting a mix of sectors with different levels of ICT use, as well as sectors that manufacture hardware and software, FEEM was able to relate an industry's tendency to cluster to its level of ICT intensity. The research included the automotive sector, financial services, electronics, computing services and communications sectors.[3]

FEEM found that ICT intensity was contributing to dispersion except in service sectors such as financial services. However, they found another force pulling in the opposite direction: sectors in which the critical assets are knowledge and learning were tending to cluster.

Where industries are already clustered at Europe's core, a high level of knowledge intensity will tend to keep them there. ICT intensity on the other hand could push industries (apart from service industries) away, leading to a larger number of clusters in a more evenly distributed pattern across Europe.

For this reason, less knowledge-intensive sectors such as motor vehicles and electronics are leaving the core to exploit cheaper land and labour costs in the periphery, while knowledge-intensive industries such as computing services remain at the core.

This is borne out by the experience of the Ruhr in Germany, Piedmont in Italy and Wales in the UK, three regions studied by FEEM for Digital Europe. Although very different in terms of size, population, economy and culture, they share a common history. All had their heyday in the industrial economy and saw their fortunes crumble in the 1970s and 1980s, with high unemployment and poor economic performance. All three are trying to adapt to and benefit from ICT in order to turn their economies around. FEEM noticed that growth in the ICT sectors in these regions was higher than the average rate of growth. Did this mean that ICT was driving the growth of new regional hubs?

FEEM's research suggested that ICT was not the deciding factor. The ICT industries were being attracted by the pre-existence of universities, cities or large companies in the region. As researcher Carole Maignan put it: 'Large firms often play an essential role in the development of a region's economy, because most large firms will have a trail of smaller companies following them. These smaller companies can be part of the larger company's value chain or they could be related companies set up by former employees from the large company. The large company acts as a driver for a cluster of companies.'

Growth in the ICT sector in these regions was not the result of ICT bringing everyone closer together no matter where they were, but because ICT is one of a number of knowledge-based industries that rely on the proximity of intellectual and human capital. The achievements of Nokia have been a spur to the entire Oulu region of Finland and led to the growth of a network of smaller companies. But Finland's success thousands of kilometres from Europe's core has had little to do with the 'death of distance' because of ICT, as the fleets of planes flying in and out of Helsinki airport, laden with 'Nokians' and their associates, attest. Oulu is a prosperous region because of the knowledge and learning built up around a large and dynamic company. As Carole says: 'Even though distances have become easier to overcome with ICT, locality still matters a great deal for companies'. Kate Oakley, associate director of the Local Futures Group in the UK, sets out the implications of this for policy makers, calling for a 'new European vision of knowledge-based development', in her contribution in box 2.1.

Box 2.1 *A new European vision of knowledge-based development*
Kate Oakley

Throughout Europe, the outlines of the digital economy are being super-imposed on those of older, industrial or agrarian economies, changing the geography of jobs and prosperity. While some European regions are still de-industrializing, others – high-tech, knowledge-intensive and metropolitan – are witnessing rising living standards and competition for well-paid jobs. And those same areas are where the physical infrastructure of the knowledge economy is concentrated, high speed broadband in particular. These areas also benefit from the supporting infrastructure of financial services (often not available in low income communities), privatized transport and select 'live/work' accommodation. In other words, it is the knowledge-based economy that is driving the take up of digital technology, not the other way round.

This fact should be of concern to European policy makers for two main reasons. Firstly, growth and development is unbalanced and there is some evidence that the gap between richer and poorer regions is growing. Secondly, while technology and infrastructure simply follow the economy, other goals such as community development, environmental improvements and enhanced democracy, will be subordinated.

Unlike other types of infrastructure, such as transport and water, digital infrastructure bears the hallmarks of its history of private and privatized development. It has largely been constructed by the market, aided and abetted by public policy, with occasional tweaks in favour of regional development or social goals. It has been formed primarily to aid commerce, to facilitate production and consumption and to serve the so-called competitive goals of the infrastructure providers. A quick comparison of the high levels of broadband access in central and west London, compared to lower levels in poorer east London, makes the point succinctly.

As Manuel Castells, professor of sociology at the University of Berkeley has noted, 'The global economy will expand in the twenty-first century, using substantial increases in the power of telecommunications and information processing... But it will do so selectively, linking valuable segments and discarding *used up, or irrelevant locales and people*.' (Italics mine) The question is, do we want parts of Europe, regions and communities, to be viewed as irrelevant in this global economy?

If the answer is no, we need to do more than put high speed broadband in all regions, though this is a start. The recent comments of European Commissioner Mario Monti suggest that the Commission is looking favourably at the case for state subsidies for broadband and mobile networks. But the only way to ensure *demand* for such networks is to combine this with a programme of social and economic development.

I stress the social because simply focusing on jobs and high-level skills – as most knowledge economy policies do, with their endless talk of high-tech incubators and science parks – will risk leaving too many European citizens on the margins. Jobs and prosperity are vital. But not only do we need to ensure that these are as widely distributed, both socially and geographically, as possible; we also need to ensure that European citizens get the chance to live happier, healthier lives. This means developing a notion of knowledge-based development that is not just about work and not just focused on science, technology and other high-growth sectors.

When we talk of the knowledge economy, we always need to ask, 'What knowledge? Whose knowledge has value? And why?'.

Opening this debate means challenging many of the underlying assumptions and myths of the digital age. These include the notion that ICT, one of the most publicly funded and supported of corporate sectors, is somehow a 'frontier' technology that needs to be kept 'free' from state 'interference'. That bridging the digital divide is something that can be left to the favours of benign corporations – with vouchers for school computers and free kit for community groups. And most fundamentally of all, that what is good for the market is automatically good for the rest of society.

It may seem a fanciful notion at the moment, given recent splits and divisions, but I believe that we desperately need a new European vision of knowledge-based development and the technology that supports it.

It should be one that is based on citizenship rights, not favours. It should recognize that not all regions are moving at the same pace and that slow-burn, local economic development should be given the same priority and even greater investment than 'big bang' globalized areas. And above all it should understand the cyberspace created by ICT as a holistic space. This is akin to older notions of the city: where all citizens have a role to play; where the focus is on communication and exchange, not just on consumption; and finally, where commerce takes place alongside all other human activities, but does not dominate.

Out of office

A man sits cross-legged on a sunny patio, wearing t-shirt and shorts, surrounded by foliage. He's holding a distinctly late-90s looking phone to his ear and simultaneously typing on a laptop computer. This archetypal vision of the teleworker of the twenty-first century appeared on the cover of a 1998 edition of *Green Futures*, the sustainable development magazine, in a special feature called 'The future of work in the virtual society'. Inside the magazine, we read that telework could mean 'more work opportunities for people living in remote communities, parents with young children, and those with disabilities'.[4]

Teleworking uses ICT to overcome distance, making your location a less important factor in your work. With fewer people making the daily commute to the office, home-based telework was seen by many as an opportunity to reduce environmental pollution from transport. And with people staying at home to work, connected to the office with a high-speed Internet link, it was also seen as a way to revive local communities. People would be able to get to know their neighbours and perhaps take part more in local community activities, reversing the distressing erosion of community life observed and decried by academics and media alike.

There is some research that suggests this is happening. For example, a study of Norwegian teleworkers in 2001 found that many were able to entertain friends, either at lunch or on weekday evenings, due to the flexibility of being at home.[5] A consultant we spoke to during research for Digital Europe said that working from home allowed him to plan his evenings better: 'When I'm working at home I'm more inclined to do something social. I can finish work at a reasonable and predictable time instead of being stuck in traffic. If I've been in the car for an hour and a half, I'm more likely to want to stay in.'[6]

Other studies have made the case for a link between home-based telework and community participation. A survey of home-based teleworkers employed by BT in the UK reported that 14 per cent found that telework made it easier for them to get involved with community activities, while less than half a per cent thought that teleworking made community involvement harder. 17 per cent of those already engaged in community activities said that they spent more time on those activities after taking up telework, with only 2 per cent saying that their time commitments had reduced.[7] This is encouraging for local communities, but we've no cause for celebration yet: the percentages in these studies are modest by any standards.

These limited gains are mirrored when we look at the evidence for environmental savings associated with working from home. Not only is travelling to work a relatively small factor in transport related carbon dioxide emissions, the behavioural changes associated with telework could actually end up having a negative effect.

The very reason why the American telecoms giant AT&T first introduced telework policies was to reduce travel related pollution, in response to the Clean Air Act in the US in 1989. The company reasoned that if a significant proportion of its employees worked from home instead of commuting to work by car, it could considerably reduce its carbon dioxide emissions. AT&T's assumption turned out to have some credence. They calculated that the telework scheme had reduced the company's carbon dioxide emissions in 2000 by 48,450 million tonnes.[8] Other companies have equally positive stories to tell. The survey of BT's teleworking staff mentioned earlier found that car users were saving 178 miles and rail users 220 miles in their weekly journey to and from work. If these figures are typical of the teleworking scheme as a whole, total savings could be as high as 424,000 miles of car travel and 190,000 miles of rail travel per week – although these figures don't include changes in non-work related travel.[9]

Company surveys on telework paint an optimistic picture of its environmental potential. But, as the transport team at the Wuppertal Institute discovered, national figures tell a different story. The team looked at Germany as an example. Despite the growing popularity of telework, the total distance travelled for commuting is actually increasing. Between 1991 and 2000, it increased year on year by 0.5 per cent per employee, with a slight dip in 2000 – caused by an increase in the price of petrol rather than any take up of telework.[10]

Karl Otto Schallaböck at the Wuppertal Institute set out to predict what the potential transport related savings of home-based telework might be: a best case scenario and a worst case scenario. In Germany, commuting accounts for almost 17 per cent of all passenger kilometres travelled. The first step was to work out the percentage of people that could work from home, as not all jobs are suited to home working. From the list of professional classifications for the German labour force, Schallaböck worked out that only 24 per cent of jobs are teleworkable from home. If all of that 24 per cent worked from home five days a week, it would save 24 per cent of commuting travel, which works out at just 4 per cent of passenger kilometres in Germany. But home-based teleworkers rarely work permanently from home. Schallaböck assumed that they spent two days a week at home, ensuring a good balance of time spent in and away from the office. This translated into a saving of only 1.6 per cent of total passenger kilometres travelled in Germany. A very sobering figure – and that's the best case scenario.

The worst case scenario takes rebound effects into consideration. Rebound effects are the indirect effects of technology use that can have negative environmental impacts, even when the direct effects of that technology appear positive. For example, when people work at home, they can't pick up shopping on the way back from the office, so they might take a break in the afternoon and make a special trip in the car. Or, because they have to commute less frequently, they may accept longer commuting distances and move further away from where they work. In theory, rebound effects could more than balance out the initial environmental savings that home-based telework creates.

History tells us that this is quite likely. A study into the evolution of passenger transport in Germany between 1950 and 1989 indicates that transport time is more or less constant. People travel further faster rather than travelling less. It's probable that teleworkers will follow this general pattern: the length of the average commute is likely to increase as the number of journeys made decreases. Schallaböck calculated that, if 24 per cent of the working population worked two days a week at home, the total distance travelled for commuting could actually rise by 2.5 per cent.

Schallaböck's calculations were based on data from Germany, but his conclusions are relevant for other European countries. Commuting accounts for 21 per cent of all kilometres travelled in Sweden and 19.5 per cent in Great Britain. Schallaböck's predictions make it clear that teleworking is not a step-change solution for the environment. To make it work for sustainable development, we need to integrate measures to accommodate this kind of flexible working into wider transport strategies and support them with change in other areas of transport provision. For example, weekly and monthly tickets on public transport offer savings to passengers who commute five days a week. They don't offer teleworkers the flexibility they require, encouraging them into their cars. Other forms of tickets could better serve their needs, such as a public transport ticket valid for any ten days in one month.

Virtual dematerialization

New economy commentator Charles Leadbeater was optimistic about ICT and a lightweight future for the economy. He wrote that: 'the innovation driven, information rich economy holds out a tantalising promise for environmentalists: economic growth with far fewer environmental side effects. In an economy in which competitiveness turns on innovation, the opportunities to design entirely new production systems that use fewer materials and energy have never been greater.'[11]

The need to break the link between economic growth and the use of resources as Leadbeater describes is urgent. Patterns of consumption and production are depleting our natural environment to a point where the planet's ability to support its human population, let alone a decent quality of life for every individual, looks seriously in doubt. Lester Brown, president of the Earth Policy Institute, brings this point home starkly:

> '*If China were to have a car in every garage, America style, it would need 80 million barrels of oil a day – more than the world currently produces. If paper consumption per person in China were to reach the US level, China would need more paper than the world produces. There go the world's forests. If the fossil fuel based, automobile centred, throwaway economic model will not work for China, it will not work for the other 3 billion people in the developing world and it will not work for the rest of the world.*'[12]

Environmental economists argue that we are moving from an era in which manufactured capital (machinery, labour) was the limiting factor, to one in which what is left of our natural capital is the limiting factor, and our behaviour needs to change accordingly. As environmental economist Hermen Daley argues: 'Instead of maximizing returns to and investing in man made capital, we must now maximize returns to and invest in natural capital'.[13] We need to shift the focus from labour productivity to resource productivity – doing more with less.

In their seminal work, *Factor Four: Doubling Wealth, Halving Resource Use*, Ernst von Weizsäcker, Amory Lovins and Hunter Lovins argue that protecting the Earth's resources demands a four-fold increase in resource productivity.[14] In other words, we need to derive four times more value from each unit of resource used. Figure 2.1 illustrates how we need to dramatically decouple use of natural resources from economic growth and quality of life to realize this factor four goal. Given that per capita consumption is about five times higher in OECD countries than in the developing world, leading environmentalist, Friedrich Schmidt-Bleek, has since proposed that resource intensity in OECD countries be reduced by a factor of ten, as he explains in box 2.2. This doesn't mean that every individual production process within the economy has to become more resource efficient by a factor of four or ten. Some sectors have more potential for resource efficiency than others. The challenge is to find out who can contribute what to make the biggest overall environmental saving.

Modern technology has a special place in the history of sustainable development, alternately being seen as the damnation of the world and as its saviour. In the first camp there are people like Edward Goldsmith, with his powerfully evoked technosphere in which humans are woefully dependent on technology, their connection with the natural world tragically and dangerously severed. In the other camp are von Weizsäcker and the Lovinses among

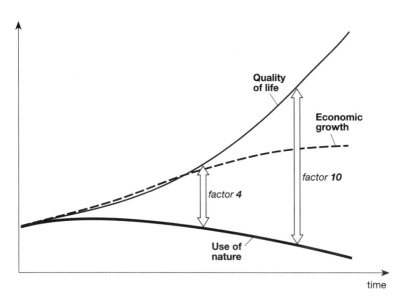

Figure 2.1 *Factor 4 and factor 10: decoupling quality of life and economic growth from use of nature*
Source: Wuppertal Institute

others, who argue that clever technological fixes are going to be vital in realizing improvements in resource productivity

We can think of environmental impacts as being a function of population, per capita consumption and the technological efficiency of consumption. Economist Paul Ehrlich expressed it in the equation, $I = P \times C \times T$, where I is environmental impact, P is population, C is per capita consumption and T is technological efficiency. With population and consumption on the increase, the onus falls on technology to make factor 4 or factor 10 improvements possible.

Optimism that ICT could break the link between consumption and resource use rested on the following assumptions:[15]

- The ICT sector is less resource intensive than traditional industrial sectors. If the sector's share of the total economy grows, overall environmental impact could fall.
- ICT could reduce the environmental impact of traditional industries by improving the efficiency of processes from procurement through to retail.

Box 2.2 *ICT: a tool for sustainability*
Friedrich Schmidt-Bleek

On average, some 30kg of non-renewable resources are needed to produce just 1kg of goods. ICT goods tend to be 10–20 times less resource
efficient than average, so that – from cradle to grave – the technical
efficiency of ICT can be less than 1 per cent. This is worrying because
hardly any product or service can be made today without a functioning
network of interconnected ICT. So as long as each product or service
draws heavily on natural capital, vital environmental systems will continue to decline.

Clearly then, western wealth is not sustainable. Firstly, at least two
planets like ours would be necessary to provide the natural resources
required if western technology was to be used by developing countries.
Secondly, we are already experiencing the consequences of our present
over-consumption of natural resources: climate change, rising ocean
levels, floods, oil spills and other events, all with economic implications.
Without massive dematerialization, therefore, humanity will move even
further from economic, social and ecological sustainability. The inter-
nationally renowned Factor 10 Club has concluded that improving
resource productivity ten-fold over the next generation is essential if we
are to reverse this.

Innovating eco-efficient technologies and consumption patterns is
needed to manage this, as is providing the social support for initiatives
that use ICT to reduce resource use.

- Certain products and services could be entirely dematerialized to create
  virtual substitutes. This could reduce their environmental impact.
- Virtual goods and services can be traded over the Internet reducing the
  volume of goods that require physical transport.
- ICT applications could also make transport infrastructure more intelligent
  and efficient, reducing the environmental load for every unit transported.

As Figure 2.2 shows, economic growth in the European Union rose between
1980 and 1997 without a corresponding increase in resource use.

The Wuppertal Institute set out to explore whether ICT had played a part
in these trends, looking for evidence to validate the first two assumptions listed
above.[16]

The first assumption was that resource savings would occur because the

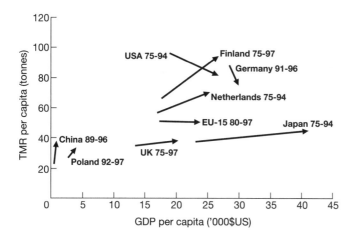

Figure 2.2 *Change in economic growth (GDP) and resource use (Total Material Requirement), between 1980–1997 in 15 EU countries*
Source: Wuppertal Institute

ICT sector itself uses relatively few resources and accounts for a growing proportion of the economy. Looking at carbon dioxide emissions and energy use as indicators, it's true that the environmental impact of the ICT sector is relatively small. For example, its contribution to direct carbon dioxide emissions and energy use is less than 1 per cent for Germany. But we need to bear in mind the sector's indirect impacts too. The ICT sector is dependent on complex networks of intermediate suppliers so we really need to look at the impacts of its entire supply chain to see the full picture. Taking these into consideration, the sector's environmental impact increases, but remains low, at around 2 per cent of carbon dioxide emissions and energy use for Germany. The ICT sector is significantly 'cleaner' per unit value added than other industry sectors, but it represents only a small share of the total economy – between 3.4 and 8.4 per cent of total gross value added (GVA), depending on statistical definition and the country in question. So, higher resource productivity in the ICT sector itself has little effect on the resource productivity of the economy as a whole at the moment, although it could be more significant in the future if the sector continues to grow.

So what is causing the increases in economy-wide resource efficiency? Looking at Germany, Italy and the UK, the most significant improvements have taken place in traditional industrial sectors. In Germany, the sectors that are most responsible for the decoupling of carbon dioxide emissions and energy use from economic growth are public administration and defence, manufacturers of chemicals and chemical products, manufacturers of base metals, and suppliers of electricity, gas, steam and hot water.

According to a survey of companies in Europe conducted by MORI for Digital Europe, 70 per cent of companies said that they were using ebusiness a fair amount or a great deal.[17] A survey for the Confederation of British Industry (CBI) in 2002 showed that the main driver for take up of ebusiness was 'operational efficiency and cost reduction'.[18]

This brings us to the second assumption in our list: that the use of ICT across industry would improve process efficiency and in doing so increase the efficiency with which resources are used. Case studies suggest that resource efficiency gains do go hand in hand with improvements in process efficiency due to ICT. Online bookseller Amazon, for example, reports that it spends 16 times less on energy than a traditional bookshop for every book sold.[19] Could it be that ICT is responsible for improvements in our environmental performance after all, not through structural change in the economy but through the use of ICT in traditional sectors?

Beyond individual case studies, it's difficult to find conclusive evidence. The team at the Wuppertal Institute looked at both overall investment in ICT and intermediate consumption of ICT goods and services, in other words, the purchase of non-durable goods and services excluding durable machine equipment. An increase in either of these in the sectors we're interested in would suggest that ICT had contributed to their improved environmental performance. Overall investment in ICT increased in Germany from €40 billion in 1991 to €60 billion in 2000, but data on ICT investment in particular sectors is not available. Sector specific data is available for the intermediate consumption of ICT goods and services, but there is no evidence of a significant increase in the sectors we're interested in. In the base metals sector, intermediate consumption of ICT rose slightly from 1.3 per cent of overall consumption in 1991 to 1.6 per cent in 1999. In the chemicals and electricity industries it remained at 2.6 and 3.7 per cent respectively throughout the 1990s.[20]

It's not illogical to assume that a world in which information, products and services can be transferred virtually will be a lightweight one. But there is currently little evidence to confirm that ICT will inevitably decouple environmental impact from consumption. Reassuringly, evidence doesn't point the other way and suggest that ICT poses an environmental threat. But, as we have seen with telework, we should be aware of the risk of rebound effects: any resource efficiency gains that we do make through the use of technology can easily be wiped out as technology frees us up to travel more, consume more and waste more.

Sustainable development in the digital society

Our research unearthed some interesting findings. But we found little evidence to allow conclusive judgements on the contribution of ICT to sustainable development at the economy-wide level. We see the same mixed picture when we look at the impacts of ICT on sustainability in business. The Digital Europe survey explored the link between a company's social and environmental impacts and its use of ebusiness applications, such as eprocurement, electronic supply chain management and elearning. From the combined responses of IT and corporate responsibility managers, we identified four categories of company according to their use of ebusiness and assessed how well each category did on sustainability measurement and sustainability performance. Companies that were defined as ebusiness leaders were more likely to measure their social and environmental impacts.[21] But we found no conclusive evidence that these companies' social and environmental indicators were actually improving simply by virtue of their use of ebusiness.[22]

We don't know exactly why ebusiness leaders are more likely to measure their environmental and social impacts. It probably has less to do with their use of ebusiness than with good, enlightened management practice. Progressive companies could be more likely to adopt ebusiness and more likely to engage with environmental and social issues.

This slightly disheartening lack of evidence seems to belie our everyday experience of how ICT is affecting our lives. Email made coordinating Digital Europe between research teams in Germany, Italy and the UK a reasonably straightforward task. We can only imagine how difficult it would have been without it. By changing the way we communicate, ICT is changing the way we work, live, build and maintain relationships. It's changing our workplaces, our communities and our institutions. In short, ICT is changing society.

We went into Digital Europe looking for changes in resource use, patterns of travel and the location of firms. But the lack of evidence in these areas and the knowledge that ICT was increasingly part of everyday life led us to look at the potential of ICT for sustainable development in a different way. This approach reflects that now being taken in the debate about the impacts of ICT on productivity, as explored by Diane Coyle in box 2.3.

We know from biological systems that the way a system is structured can itself create particular outcomes. Systems thinker Fritjof Capra described this as: 'the pattern of organization of a living system… the configuration of relationships among the system's components that determines the system's essential characteristics'.[23] Looking at the features of a system tells us a lot about the outcomes we can expect. The system in this case is human society.

At the moment society doesn't work for sustainable development – quite the reverse. Consumption fuels production, which fuels even greater consumption in the developed world, straining the planet's limited resources and robbing individuals in the developing world of their chance of a decent quality of life.

The introduction of ICT into society is changing the way it works. It's not just that we email our friends rather than sending them a letter. Embedding electronic networks, in particular the Internet and mobile, into our social networks changes the quality of the system, giving the digital society particular features. We need to understand these features – networks, information, trust and speed – if we want to understand how to make the net work for sustainable development.

Box 2.3 *Measuring the new economy*
Diane Coyle

The cost of computational power has been falling at an average of 55 per cent a year for half a century, the most dramatic and sustained decline in the price of a new technology ever recorded.[24] It would be astonishing if this weren't causing radical change in the economy and society. The difficulty with living through it is trying to assess what's happening, and what's important, without the benefit of hindsight and perhaps even without the right metrics.

One reason for the density of the informational fog is the fact that so many important economic variables are 'intangible' and ill measured: human capital, social capital, organizational change, even the output of services. There have been many ways of describing the type of change that is transforming the economy, such as new paradigm or knowledge economy, all rather imprecise, holographic even: the patterns at first glance seem clear but it's impossible to grab hold of them.

Nevertheless, it's now very obvious that the source of value added in the leading economies has changed during the past 20 years or so. All have seen a steady shift away from manufacturing to services. Even within manufacturing, value is added less and less by the physical manipulation of raw materials, more and more by innovation, design, creativity, customization and so on. Thanks to miniaturization and the use of lighter materials, the physical mass of the goods we use has diminished steadily. Some years ago I described this as the 'weightless economy',[25] a metaphor that has turned out to be literally true. Real GDP in the UK rose 29 per cent in the 1980s and the material mass of the resources used in creating it (including waste), 15 per cent. In the 1990s real GDP increased by 25 per cent but the weight of the economy by only 2 per cent.[26]

This is an economy very different from the era of mass production it is replacing and a book such as this, drawing out some of the implications, is extremely welcome. Most economists have focused on aggregate productivity figures, on the grounds that a life-transforming technology ought to show up in our basic measure of economic output. And indeed for some countries, especially the US, it has, since about 1995. But there are many reasons for thinking that important aspects of the change will never actually reach the headline GDP figures. One of these is the question of how to measure change.

One well-known problem in measuring change is the failure of GDP to capture the welfare benefits of new goods, greater variety and step-changes in technology. Although we are used to the ways in which GDP overstates welfare, for example by ignoring environmental costs, there are also important ways in which it massively understates welfare. The most important of these is anything that improves health or longevity, as biotechnology will.[27] Going beyond these old problems with GDP, the metrics we have for economic well-being might well have to change more profoundly in the weightless economy. The very concept of the 'output' of a service is often troubling.[28] After all, you can't stockpile operations or mortgages. Supply is defined by demand.

We will need to look more at statistics on consumption rather than production. Time use statistics may reveal patterns of change faster than conventional figures, as they reflect real consumption, ignoring the boundary between market and non-market transactions. This boundary is shifting as cheaper information costs extend the reach of markets and increase the value of other activities that are too complex and sophisticated to be bought and sold in the marketplace.[29]

Official statisticians have recognized this and are starting to collect time use data more systematically, with the US Bureau of Labor Statistics launching an annual survey and funding a research programme. It may be that the most immediate impact of ICT on our lives, the reason we really know the economy has changed, is the astonishing sense of time pressure everybody feels. It's a long way from conventional macro-economics and productivity gains, but the combination of always rushing – and yet living far longer – may well turn out to be strong signals of economic transformation.

In the process of integrating the different research strands of the Digital Europe project, we discovered something entirely different about the contribution of ICT to sustainable development, beyond economy-wide changes in sustainable development indicators. The rest of the book looks at the features of the digital society and explores how we might use them to build a more sustainable world for this and future generations.

The first feature we'll look at is networks – the underlying structure of society as well as the structure underpinning the use of ICT. We'll explore what happens when social networks move on to electronic platforms.

NETTING THE GLOBE

In Mainz, southern Germany, on 30 September 1452, a full 500 years after printing presses with movable clay type were first used in China, Johannes Gutenberg published his celebrated Bible using a printing press with movable metal type. This medieval revolution in ICT took several decades to spread around Europe, arriving in Basle in 1466, Rome in 1467 and Paris three years later. It wasn't until 1476 that William Caxton opened the first printing press in London, and Moscow didn't see its benefits until 1555.

Compare the spread of the printing press in the middle ages to that of a more modern innovation, the 'tamagotchi', the virtual pet toy designed and marketed in Japan by Bandai Inc. The tamagotchi was a small computer-generated chicken-like creature that needed feeding, cleaning and cheering up on a regular basis. Owners who neglected their electronic pet would find themselves with a dead tamagotchi on their hands.

The toy was launched in Japan in November 1996 and was an instant success with teenagers. The fad spread from school to school, via word of mouth, email and a vast number of websites set up to discuss the treatment of tamagotchis. By the spring of 1997 it was selling out in toyshops in Europe and America.

There are many social, political and economic reasons behind the gradual dispersal of the printing press and the much more rapid spread of the tamagotchi. One is simply that things move faster these days, because we're better connected – better networked.

The spread of inventions, ideas and fads sheds light on how networks function. The network is one of the very basic patterns of organization in living systems. 'At all levels of life – from the metabolic networks of cells to the food webs of ecosystems – the components and processes of living systems are interlinked in network fashion.'[1] In very basic terms, networks are made up of nodes and links. In a transport network, the nodes could be cities and the links the roads, railways and air routes that connect them; in a social network, nodes are people, and links the relationships between them.

Ideas like the tamagotchi can move so quickly across the world because every human being is part of the vast social network of human life. Everyone is connected through their relationships with other people; even prisoners in solitary confinement are connected, through the warden who brings their food, or through the letters they send and receive. Ideas spread by jumping from one person to the next, moving around the world from node linking to node linking to node.

If all people had the same number of links and were only linked to the people close to them, it would take a very long time for ideas to spread. But in reality it happens a lot faster, because some people are super connected: they have a large number of contacts and – more importantly – have relationships with people beyond their immediate circle. These super-connected people are network hubs.

It was an experiment conducted by Yale psychologist Stanley Milgram in 1967 that led to the realization that such hubs transform human social networks. Milgram randomly selected 300 people living in Omaha, Nebraska in the US and instructed them to get a letter to a target person in Boston using only personal contacts. Knowing only the name, location and occupation of the target person, the participants had to forward the letter to someone they thought was more likely to know the target. The process was repeated until the letters arrived at their intended destination. Of the 60 letters that eventually got there, on average each had been through only 6 pairs of hands. In a country of around 200 million people, how could total strangers be linked by only 6 degrees? This was the question that puzzled network theorists when they looked at Milgram's research. They soon realized that it was all down to the role of hubs. By linking people in distant parts of the network, hubs were creating short paths between seemingly unconnected individuals. This feature of social networks is known as the 'small world' phenomenon.

In 1973, Mark Granovetter was the first sociologist to distinguish between different types of links in human networks. He argued that people tend to have two different kinds of links with each other, a large number of 'strong links' to family and friends and then a small number of connections with people further afield that are known as 'weak links'.[2] Some people have more weak links than others and these people are the hubs within the social network. As more and more of our social interaction takes place electronically, ICT will affect how these links are created and maintained.

The number of people with access to ICT is growing rapidly, allowing people and groups of people to connect more easily with others. In September 2002, there were an estimated 606 million Internet users and rising, with the Internet present in the majority of offices and schools and a good proportion of homes in Europe.[3] Even more startling are the figures for mobile phone ownership. Around one in five people in the world currently uses a mobile phone and this is forecast to rise to one in three by 2005: over 2 billion users.[4]

This process of 'netting the globe' isn't happening at an even rate from country to country and it's by no means a foregone conclusion that the entire world will be connected without significant effort. Despite the worldwide popularity of mobile phones, penetration in Africa is still less than 2 per cent.[5] But it's clear that human systems are increasingly being mediated over electronic networks. Changing the way that people connect changes the qualities of the network and so changes the way that society functions. David Weinberger speculates about the extent to which this could transform social networks in box 3.1.

Box 3.1 *Global conversations*
David Weinberger

The Internet is the largest and most accessible information space ever constructed. People can now find out pretty much anything that we humans have learned in our time on this Earth. It would be hard to overestimate the importance of this new capability.

Yet, something more is going on.

The Internet has already gone far beyond information. The Internet removes the barriers to publishing and finding content, but it also enables two-way communication. But 'communication' is too dry a word. 'Communication' sounds like two information-processing entities exchanging bits, when in fact the Internet has enabled hundreds of millions of global *conversations*. In fact, we're inventing new ways of conversing at a remarkable pace: email, mailing lists, discussion boards, chat, instant messaging, blogs (weblogs) and whatever is invented tomorrow. And each of these new conversational modes has its own distinct types: it hardly seems fair to lump together the reflective discussions of a university theology department with the cutting rhetoric of Slashdot.org just because both are threaded discussions.

Inventing new ways of conversing is no small thing and used to only happen rarely. The last time was when we invented the telephone. Conversations consist of people turning towards the world together and nothing is more basic than that. Furthermore, conversations occur between people who are speaking in their own voices about what matters to them. They are fundamental both to our societies and to who we are as individuals. Enabling a new global conversation is a big deal.

But something more is going on.

Unlike conversations on telephones, Internet-based conversations can have permanence. They can even have their own place; the web makes this especially easy. As a result, the conversations aren't mere words beating in air. They endure and gather groups around them. There are mailing lists well into their second decade and there are websites that are likely to live at the same address for entire lifetimes. These groups vary widely in every way: number of members, membership requirements, expectations of comport-ment, frequency of interaction. They generally shape themselves to the customs and interests of their participants, unlike most real world groups that start with a constitution or a charter of some sort.

But something more is going on.

Groups that form around conversations and that persist over time often grow thick, complex relationships among their participants. The members get to know one another. Rather than being held together by a shared inter-est, the group may become held together by the members' shared interest in one another. Such groups, in the real world or online, are messy, ambiguous and rich in what makes humans an interesting species.

But something more is going on.

As these messy groups overlap and entwine, convoluted, untraceable webs form. This is precisely what happened with blogs. They started out as ways to share information: a geek would list which websites he or she had visited that day. As bloggers started replying to other blogs, they became conversations. Over time, bloggers started linking to the other blogs they read and had conversed with. These mini webs of blogs form amorphous, shifting groups of people getting to know one another better everyday. And it's not just happening with blogs.

Something more is going on.

Connect these blog webs to the rest of the Internet sprawl. We're talking with a wider range of people from around the world through all the conver-sational forms we're busy inventing. It's not just the conversations that endure. The links do too. The links are human relationships. As a result, we're living online now in the midst of a set of human connections that are complex, unmanageable, unpredictable and deeply satisfying. In other words, what began as an information space has now become a world.

And a world is a lot more than an information space.

We don't yet know what to make of this world. No generation has grown up in it. Connections are still intermittent and slow compared with what they will be. Accessibility tracks along the usual dismal economic topology. We are just beginning to inhabit this new world, a world that is entirely of our inventing. But the basic nature of this world is visible already: its geog-raphy consists of links among people that are as twisty and variegated as people themselves. The existence of this new, public world is itself a 'some-thing more', a gift that we have given ourselves.

In his influential trilogy on the 'Information Age', Manuel Castells wrote that: 'a new society emerges when and if a structural transformation can be observed in the relationships of production, in the relationships of power and in the relationships of experience. These transformations lead to an equally substantial modification of social forms of space and time, and to the emergence of a new culture.' Castells calls this new culture the 'network society'.[6]

Could the new network society, or the digital society as we have called it, be more in tune with the goals of sustainable development? In the rest of this chapter we'll look at the environmental and social impacts of connecting everyone and argue that there could be significant social benefits if we can make the network as inclusive as possible. But this will require more network infrastructure, so every effort must be made to improve its environmental efficiency. We'll also see how networks in business affect the ability of companies to contribute to sustainable development and the ability of NGOs and campaigners to influence business. The chapter ends by suggesting that the most significant contribution to sustainable development may come from the creation of a highly networked world in which the positive values we hold as individuals can be expressed at a global scale.

The Internet begins with coal – but where does it end?

Netting the globe means more network infrastructure, more access devices, a proliferation of manufactured 'stuff'. And it also means more energy to keep the whole thing running. But knowing exactly what those energy demands are is tricky. For example, the Internet comprises PCs, servers, routers, switches, cables and so on. We can say that Internet servers and routers are definitely Internet infrastructure and nothing else, but what about PCs? People don't use their PCs just to access the Internet, so any calculation on the energy use of the Internet has to make assumptions about what proportion of PC time is Internet time. It's even trickier when thinking about the applications of the Internet, such as ecommerce. Should the energy used to transport goods bought over the Internet be factored into the overall equation? Not to mention the effect of widespread Internet use on whole economies and the efficiency with which they are run.

One of the first sorties into this contentious field was made in an article in *Forbes* magazine back in 1999, entitled, 'The Internet begins with coal'. The authors suggested that Internet use accounted for as much as 13 per cent of the total energy used in the US and that increased usage would swell this eventually to a massive 50 per cent. Oddly, the article didn't call for restrictions in use of the Internet or concerted action to increase energy efficiency, but for construction of a number of new (fossil-fuel burning) power stations.

As it turns out, the figures used in the calculations featured in that article were drawn from top-of-the-range estimates for the energy use of all components – and were supplied by a coal lobby group.[7]

Later, more balanced analysis seemed to suggest that the correct figure for the proportion of total energy used in the US was more like 1 per cent.[8] The Wuppertal Institute has looked at the energy demands of Internet use in Germany. They found that in 2000, the Internet accounted for about 1 per cent of Germany's total energy use and could rise to about 5 per cent by 2010. This rise is due to projections of greater use of the Internet and to changes in the standards that govern it.[9]

At the moment, the Internet is governed by a set of technical standards for computer-to-computer communication called Internet Protocol version 4, or IPv4, but very soon this set of standards is likely to be replaced by IPv6. The problem with the current system is that it only allows a limited number of Internet Protocol (IP) addresses and you need an IP address if you want access to the Internet. There's a total of 4.3 billion IPv4 addresses available, which seems like a lot, but two thirds have already been used up and the number of people wanting to go online keeps on growing. What's more, IP addresses were doled out somewhat unevenly to different institutions and countries. All the institutions in China put together have fewer IP addresses allocated to them than many single American universities.

IPv6 will expand the number of addresses to make it almost unlimited, so China and other countries like it won't have to worry about this aspect of getting their citizens online. Those behind IPv6 are right in calling it a social project. But it will create enough IP addresses not just for every person in the world to have their own, but for IP addresses to be allocated to countless inanimate objects: the fabled Internet toaster and Internet fridge, but also the Internet car, the Internet curtains, the Internet pair of shoes and the Internet pizza box. Tiny chips embedded everywhere will communicate with each other using the wireless Internet, summoning into being the heralded 'ever-net'.

As an early indication of the environmental impact of pervasive computing, the Swiss Federal Laboratories for Materials Testing and Research (EMPA) got together with the German Institute for Future Studies (IZT) and estimated the impact that 'smart homes' – pervasive computing in the home – could have on electricity consumption in Switzerland. A high-tech scenario in which all objects in the home are connected to the Internet would result in a 7 per cent increase in current total electricity consumption. A more cautious scenario that supported pervasive computing in the home without connecting every gadget to the Internet, would result in a 1.2 per cent increase.[10]

The German-Swiss study points out that indirect effects could well offset the direct environmental effects of pervasive computing in the home. For example, it may be possible to save more energy through Internet-controlled heating systems than is used to connect the heating system to the Internet in the first place. Equally, rebound effects could wipe out direct energy savings if easy access to the Internet encourages greater consumption. This makes it important to look beyond the direct environmental impacts and consider the indirect impacts, positive and negative, of widespread ICT use. We need to look at the digital society as a whole to develop strategies for resource efficiency.

But Professor Lorenz Hilty at EMPA believes that the energy impact of the pervasive network is not the major issue. He's much more worried about the problems that could be created by embedding tiny chips into non-ICT products, such as clothing or packaging. To be able to recycle a product you need to separate out the different materials it contains. Embedded chips will be so small that when products enter the waste stream it could be almost impossible to locate the chips and remove them so the rest of the product can be recycled. If we want to reduce the material intensity of the economy, re-cycling on a large scale is vital. Embedded chips could severely hamper progress.

Networks of opportunity

The need to manage the environmental impacts of electronic networks comes from the economic and social imperative to give everyone access.

As the number of nodes in a network goes up, the value of the network rises disproportionately. Think of telephones. One on its own is completely useless; two telephones in a network have severely limited value. Start adding to that and the number of different connections that can be made over the network goes up very quickly. What has become known as Metcalfe's Law, or the net-work effect, says that, where a network consists of lots of one-to-one links, its value is equivalent to the square of the number of nodes that network con-tains. Adding just one more telephone user to a network of 20,000 users increases the number of potential connections by around 40,000.

Of course, this also works in reverse. As the value of the network rises, the disadvantage of being excluded from it also rises. The simple result of this is that, in theory, as electronic networks are used more and more to mediate social networks, people who are excluded from using electronic networks suffer disproportionately. So the imperative to give individuals access to ICT will remain strong, even if the percentage of people excluded looks small.

There are individual and wider social benefits of joining the network, but not everyone benefits equally. We mentioned earlier in this chapter that links in social networks can be either strong or weak. Strong and weak don't refer to how good or bad the links are but the regularity and depth of contact. We have strong links with people we see often, with whom we share interests, experiences and backgrounds. We have weak links with people we see less often – casual friends and acquaintances for example – and they tend to be different from us. Strong links usually work as support networks in times of difficulty or dependency, in particular for the very young or very old. Weak links give us access to different ideas and so can deliver social and economic advantage. For example, Granovetter's original research found that people were more likely to find a job through weak links, which were able to provide access to new contacts and sources of information, than through strong links. People sharing strong links had common interests and contacts, meaning that information from one strong link was much the same as that from another and so unlikely to introduce any new opportunities.

Weak links and the advantages that flow from them are not distributed evenly throughout the network. The hubs in the network, such as a successful journalist or trade union leader, enjoy unrivalled access to weak links, giving them competitive advantage over others in the network. In contrast, marginalized individuals such as the long-term unemployed tend to lack access to weak links, relying on strong ties, often to other marginalized individuals. They are the 'network poor' – 'individuals who do not have the kind of social network configuration that is most appropriate for the stage of life they have reached, to enable them to thrive'.[11]

Can the use of electronic networks to mediate social relationships give people new opportunities to build and maintain weak links, creating a more inclusive network or, in other words, can ICT build a more inclusive society?

Technology operates in a social context, so it should come as no surprise that an individual's ability to benefit from ICT is in part determined by existing social structures and opportunities. The hubs in the system are well placed to use ICT to make their weak links work harder, reinforcing their competitive advantage over others in the network. So it's possible that ICT will actually exacerbate existing inequalities in society.

But at the same time ICT does have the potential to make social networks more inclusive by creating new channels through which individuals can build and maintain weak links. What does this mean practically? It's very easy to establish contact with new people using email or through chat rooms and blogs. For some people, this additional channel for making new relationships can be very enabling. Zak, an American high school pupil, set up a blog to share his artwork, songs and poetry with others, in the hope that it would make him more popular at school. In an interview with *Newsweek* magazine, Zak explained, 'I thought people would like me if they truly knew me'. A year on, his blog has 28 daily readers and Zak feels people now see him more as he is.[12]

ICT can also help to prevent weak links from being eroded. In a case study for Digital Europe with Vodafone, we reviewed a number of studies of how people were using mobile phones. These suggested that mobiles were helpful in maintaining both strong and weak links.[13] For example, mobiles are used in the Philippines to keep the large migrant worker population in close contact with friends and family back home: 100 million text messages are sent daily. The texting helps to maintain intimacy within families (maintaining strong links) and softens the effects of culture shock and isolation that can often be felt by migrant workers.

Mobiles are also being used extensively by the deaf and hard of hearing community. According to the UK-based Royal National Institute for Deaf People, text messaging with standard mobile phones has largely replaced the previous methods of remote communication between deaf people. Email is a close second. These media give deaf people the ability to communicate remotely on equal terms with hearing people for the first time, helping to maintain weak links.

But widespread access to ICT can only ever be a first step to a more inclusive social network. We also need to equip people with the skills to succeed in the digital society, a society in which weak and strong links are mediated partly – but never wholly – by ICT. In the transition from the industrial to the information society, citizens needed new skills: finding, filtering and organizing information. These are still relevant, but education should focus more on new network competencies. The ability to create, maintain, use and contribute to social networks, together with the capacity for strategic and visionary thought and the ability to deal with diversity and change, are the keys to success in the digital society.[14]

The notion of a 'digital divide' – the divide between those with access to ICT and those without – can be misleading when considering the importance of the use of ICT in society. The concept implies that it's simply a question of being in or out of the digital society. But getting online or buying a mobile is just the first step to 'digital inclusion' and it's quite likely that people will find themselves in a similar state of disadvantage after joining the network as they were before.

In another case study for Digital Europe, we argued that we should think less of a digital divide and more in terms of a 'digital ladder' with numerous rungs. At the very top of the ladder are the 'digerati'. They may not be the ones who build the technology and write the software programs, but they have the knowledge, skills and connections to use ICT to maintain their position as the hubs in the network society. A rung further down are the 'professionals'. For them ICT is a work tool, an information tool and a net-working tool. Moving further down, 'online novices' derive some benefit from the network but are limited by poor technological literacy. At the bottom of the ladder are the offliners, excluded from the benefits of ICT but not immune from wider socio-economic change.[15]

Where does this leave us? Society is 'tooling up', using ICT more and more to enhance and support social networks. The network form could lead to increasing divisions in society between people with lots of weak links – hubs – and people without access to the technology or the skills to benefit from it. But giving people cheap, reliable access to ICT and the skills and confidence to be active participants in the network society could help them build and maintain weak links, creating a more inclusive network. An inclusive network moves us one step closer to making the digital society work for sustainable develop-ment.

Networks in business

In the early 1990s Nokia was a failing conglomerate producing everything from toilet paper, rubber boots and car tyres, to cables, computers and tele-visions. Today it's one of the world's leading mobile communications com-panies. In *The Finnish Model* Manuel Castells and fellow Berkeley sociologist, Pekka Himanen, identified Nokia's shift to become a network enterprise as key to its successful transformation. They argued that it got ahead of the pack by collaborating closely with suppliers, competitors and research organiza-tions on product development, market trend analysis and so on.[16] The success of Spanish clothing manufacturer, Zara, a new entrant in the high street fash-ion industry in the late 1990s, can also be put down to networks. It has imple-mented a system that directly links information on sales in stores to designers and manufacturers, allowing information on consumer preferences to dictate the direction of future product strategy, taking new designs from pattern to peg in two weeks. According to Castells and Himanen: 'Networks have extra-ordinary advantages as organizing tools because of their inherent flexibility and adaptability, critical features in order to survive in a fast changing environment'.[17]

Understanding networks makes us better placed to challenge the sustain-able development performance of business. Given the limited resources of NGOs and campaigners, it is the companies with most to lose – those with big consumer-facing brands – that are most in the spotlight. When social and environmental misdemeanors are picked up in the supply chain, it tends to be these companies that come under fire. Their need to protect the value of their brand makes them in turn more responsive to pressure. The brand is a two-way communication tool between company and customer and when customers begin to abandon a brand because of some perceived breach of trust, companies listen.

However, many large companies don't have massive consumer-facing brands, because they don't need them. They sell to corporate customers only and with a limited number of clients employ account managers to do the talking instead. One example is BT Global Services, the business-to-business (B2B) arm of the UK telecoms giant, with an annual turnover of £5 billion and a corporate client base of around 5,000. Other examples are Cisco, Lucent Technologies or the metal company, Corus.

Taking a network-based approach might allow corporate responsibility issues to get to this kind of company. This could be an interesting exercise to try (if you have a bit of time on your hands): draw a map of all the consumer-facing brands in, say, the ICT sector. Identify their key suppliers and draw the links between the different companies. Very soon a network pattern will emerge on the map and in that network will be hubs: B2B companies supplying vast numbers of other companies with a range of goods, connected through networks of trade. Repeat the exercise for another sector and almost certainly some of the same companies will appear as hubs. These hubs suddenly look as if they wield extraordinary influence in the economy, through the products they supply and the number of connections they have. Exerting influence to improve social and environmental practices here, perhaps through consortia of clients, could make a significant impact on business across the board.

Sustainable development in a small world

Campaigners have followed business and turned to the flexibility of networks to increase the efficiency with which they can mobilize in the interests of sustainable development. In the past, it was difficult to coordinate global campaigns. Now, local groups continue to campaign on local issues, but it's easier to bring the full weight of a global network to bear on issues of global concern. ICT has transformed loosely connected groups of campaigners passionate about human rights into an effective campaign network able to coordinate reaction to global human rights abuses.

While these high profile campaign networks can be effective, in the end the wider shift to a more networked society could promote a better response from the corporate sector to sustainable development. Technology facilitates the formation of a greater number of weak links into distant parts of the network, creating the 'small world' effect. This could create a system in which we are better equipped to pursue sustainable development.

The pupils at Taylorsville Elementary in North Carolina, USA, wanted to see how fast and how far emails spread, so they each sent an email to all of their friends and family requesting them to forward the message to everyone they knew. In addition, each recipient was told to respond to the pupils directly so they could keep a record of how far the email had spread. The experiment was abandoned after the pupils received 450,000 responses from every state in the USA and 83 other countries. What the pupils hadn't realized was that they were connected, not only to their immediate family and friends, but also to everyone else on the planet, by an average of only six degrees of separation. In this kind of small world we can see the impacts of our actions even when they occur on the other side of the world.

As Ian Christie explains in box 3.2, the tradition of thought and practice associated with sustainable development has long emphasized the importance of empathy. People living in prosperity and in relatively healthy environments need to be continually reminded of the plight of other people, the billions living in poverty or surrounded by devastated environments. Only if those with most power to act maintain empathy, can we build momentum around sustainable development. A paper written by Chris Tuppen, head of Sustainable Development and Corporate Accountability at BT, and Jonathon Porritt made the following point, linking the values that underpin the idea of sustainable development to the need for global feedback mechanisms:

'*Values can be thought of as agreed rules that enable the smooth running of society; they aren't agreed by committee or imposed on societies from above. They emerge from the collective behaviour of individuals and respond to the needs of societies as a whole. For this system to function a feedback mechanism needs to be in place; people need to be able to see the effects of their actions on others. In a small community, this is a straightforward process. But sustainable development is a global problem and the effects of our actions are often indirect, taking place thousands of miles away. For values to develop that are aligned to sustainable development, adequate feedback mechanisms are required – mechanisms that nurture empathy, that allow us to witness global problems and connect them to their cause.*'[18]

Box 3.2 *Empathy matters*
Ian Christie

'*As …the gulfs of wealth and power among us [widen], we need imagination, metaphor and empathy more than ever, to help us remember each other's essential humanity. I believe this will be the central challenge of the coming century – one that will shape everything else about who we are and what we become.*' Thomas Homer-Dixon, *The Ingenuity Gap.*[19]

From a sustainability perspective, modern industrial development has neglected three vast constituencies, with possibly fatal consequences to them and also to the rich world:

- the billion or so 'absolute poor' who have been left far behind in the development of the global South; and the 'underclass' poor of the rich world;
- the unborn generations who will inherit an ecologically ravaged planet if worst case scenarios for climate disruption and loss of biodiversity prove to be accurate;
- many thousands of species of wildlife vulnerable to loss of habitat, changes in the environment and climate, and over-exploitation for human consumption.

It takes an act and effort of imagination and will to achieve fellow feeling for any of these. The act of imagining ourselves into another's situation is empathy. It is one of the fundamental features of a mature and healthy social life and rounded identity. A gross lack of empathy often marks people who commit the worst acts of violence and abuse. Empathy comes most readily to us when putting ourselves in the place of those most like us; it is hardest for us when confronted with people or species that we feel are wholly 'other'.

Empathy is something we have to struggle for in many cases. The tide of information that flows over us, the multiple causes crying out for support, the ease with which we brutally generalize about people with whom we disagree or are fighting, our ignorance about other ways of life, the vast gap between the lives of the poorest and those of the affluent and very rich...all these make empathy hard to gain and hold on to. But it is essential to the task of sustainable development. We have to see the remote poor, the unborn generations and endangered species as part of our circle of concern and fellow-feeling if an ethic of sustainability is to develop and endure. How can this happen?

Tools for the generation of empathy

As the quotation from Thomas Homer-Dixon above implies, finding ways to foster empathy in a deeply divided world is one of the deepest challenges we face. The 'toolkit' for generating empathy, however, is more varied and potent than ever before:

- The mass media can be a force for division, ignorance and prejudice, particularly where ownership is concentrated among moguls with a narrow political agenda. But the emergence of the Internet is opening up new channels for debate and exchange of ideas and information across all kinds of barriers.

- Computer simulation technology has been used to take us into fantasy environments – as in films such as 'The Matrix'. Could it be used to take us further into real environments – exploring shared problems and scenarios based on detailed computer-assisted analyses and representations of our worlds?
- The evolution of new techniques for consensus-building and conflict resolution is potentially of great significance. In South Africa, the end of apartheid and a relatively peaceful transition to majority rule were helped by the imaginative use of scenario planning to generate common cause for the future between blacks and whites, and by the Truth and Reconcilation Commission, a model being copied elsewhere.
- 'Meeting differently' can open up the horizons and understanding of decision makers, whose elite lifestyles are shielded from unsustainable realities behind heavy security and the cosseted environment of global summits and business conferences. We will be making real progress when the G8 summits move from pampered hideaways to more imaginative and grittier forms of involvement in debate with people in the world's most deprived, unsustainable and salutary settings.

'Seeing is believing'. When we meet and debate 'differently', there is a chance of having a new perspective on people and problems. Finding imaginative ways to bring people into encounters with 'others' – the distant poor at home and abroad, the unborn and other species – is an essential complement to, and often a precondition for, developing powerful policies to harness more sustainable technologies and market forces. Sustainable development calls for a distinctive emotional intelligence. Sustainable developers need to be 'empathy enablers'.

In a networked system such as that emerging now, we can think of this empathy as negative feedback (see box 3.3). The problems the planet faces have been caused by a complex system failing or going out of control. The economy grows, using up more natural capital, and as it grows it generates more growth and more consumption, hurtling fast forward in a positive feedback loop. Negative feedback – facilitated by empathy – is what is needed to regulate the system and restore equilibrium.

For the system to support sustainable development, it needs to have the capacity for negative feedback on a global scale. Electronic networks could be

---

Box 3.3 *Positive and negative feedback*

A feedback loop is a circular pattern of causally connected elements, in which each element has an effect on the next, until the last feeds back into the first element. Feedback loops are a feature of the network patterns that characterize living systems and allow living systems to be self-regulating. According to the direction of change, feedback can be 'negative' or 'positive'.[20]

Positive feedback is self-reinforcing: one element reinforces the effect of another.

Perhaps the simplest example of positive feedback is what happens when a microphone is placed too close to a speaker. If the microphone picks up a sound, it's amplified and broadcast by the loudspeaker. The broadcast sound is then picked up again by the microphone, amplified and broadcast again, and so on, until the sound is deafening. Nothing is regulating the positive feedback. As this example shows, positive doesn't necessarily mean good.

Negative feedback is self-balancing: one element counterbalances the effect of another.

A classic example of the use of negative feedback is in Watt's steam engine. Watt created a device he called a governor to regulate the amount of steam produced by an engine. Two balls are attached to the top of a rod by hinges. The steam drives the rod and as the rod spins the balls fly outwards and upwards: the faster the steam, the higher the balls. As the balls rise, they close off a valve, slowing the steam.

---

providing this feedback mechanism, connecting people and organizations to the consequences of their actions. And ICT also increases the power of empathy, allowing people to take immediate action, by signing an email list, or starting one, or organizing a protest. Few individuals will bring about change on their own. By connecting people up, ICT can create the scale needed for action to bring about change.

There is another interesting way that the network structure of the digital society may be equipping us for the challenge of sustainable development.

How many people have found themselves working for companies whose values are completely different from their own? How often do employees find themselves having to leave their values at home when they go to work and pick them up again when they return, in the meantime tolerating behaviour in their name that they would never tolerate in themselves or in a friend?

In a traditional hierarchical structure, where decisions are made at the top and handed down and nothing is handed back up in return, this situation is possible. Top down hierarchies allow values to be imposed on organizations with little recourse.

In a network structure, top down impositions are less effective, as employees can talk to each other by email – not just one to one, but by using email lists they can make it a many to many conversation. If the company does something unpopular, employees can organize protests, or more likely, gather together to suggest policies that are more aligned with their values.

Christian Seelos, manager of CSR at BT Global Services and a long time student of biological systems, has observed this phenomenon and thinks something significant is happening:

> '*In my view, the concerns underlying CSR are nothing new. But this is not the point. What is new is the scale of it. Mainly through ICT developments that allow for real time, cheap, penetrating and broad communication, small-scale efforts have gone through an inflection point. The hurdles to people orchestrating their efforts and voicing their concerns have totally scaled down – everyone is participating. The CSR movement is thus a classic emerging property of the hugely expanded communications network that has created a very complex stakeholder system totally changing the framework for actions of global businesses. To hope that this will go away is a dangerous illusion.*'

According to Christian Seelos, CSR is an example of individual values being expressed on a grander scale. It's possible that the kind of super connectivity that is becoming normal in some parts of the world is allowing this to happen.

ICT provides the connectivity that could help in building a consensus that sustainable development is a necessary goal. It has created new structures of human organization that allow values – such as those that are aligned with sustainable development – to be expressed in large organizations, not because the organizations have a benevolent leader, but because that is what employees, or consumers, or citizens want. The flatter network structure and the greater connectivity of people in the network make this possible for the first time.

The network gives the digital society an underlying structure that can work for sustainable development. But we won't make the net work just by connecting people. There's no point in having feedback mechanisms in place if there is nothing to feed back. Without information flowing on the network, from node to node, this feature of the digital society is just a structure and nothing more.

The next chapter looks in detail at how the Internet is bringing us a step closer to realizing the universal right to seek, receive and impart information regardless of frontiers. But in a society awash with information, isn't there a risk of being overwhelmed?

INFOWORLD

Lukshmi is a young woman living in a fishing village in India. Every morning she travels to the Internet cafe in a neighbouring town and downloads a detailed local weather forecast from a US Navy website. Back at her village, she announces the forecast over the public tannoy to local fishermen, giving them information about fishing conditions that they never had access to before. Thanks to the entrepreneurial spirit of one woman and cheap, easy access to information via the Internet, the fishermen are now able to make informed choices about how safe it is to take their boats out.

It's a story told by Anuradha Vitacchi, founding director of OneWorld.net, an online civil society network. She emphasizes the significance of the Internet in delivering information to ordinary people in developing countries. 'What we, the people, didn't have was a medium that gave us power – not power over anyone else, but power to pull down the content we wanted; and to become producers of the content we preferred, and to distribute it to whoever we wished. A horizontal, circular, inclusive medium that empowered all of us, in a global human network.'[1]

The Internet brings us a step closer to realizing a commitment enshrined in the UN Declaration of Human Rights over half a century ago: the right to seek, receive and impart information regardless of frontiers. There's no doubt that ICT can be remarkably empowering. For the fishermen in Lukshmi's village, it could mean the difference between life and death.

The availability of information is vital to the progress of sustainable development. The first pictures of Earth from space prompted many people to think consciously about the responsibility of human society to the environment for the first time. ICT is critical in collecting and delivering information about the plight of the planet. Many of the changes that threaten our long-term survival, such as global warming and loss of biodiversity, would go unnoticed if not for our sophisticated communications networks. What's more, powerful computers have allowed environmental scientists to develop the climate change models that give us a better understanding of global warming and its effects. ICT is used to collect, collate and communicate the data that provides evidence of environmental decline from the amount of rainforest being cleared in Brazil, to the level of greenhouse gas emissions in Europe and ultraviolet radiation in Antarctica.

But the significance of information in the digital society goes far beyond information specifically about the environment. Information is what flows on the network and it can take many different forms. It's the content of websites, it's conversations in chat rooms, it's email communication and it's text messages. We have never had access to more information. This in itself is hugely significant. But more importantly, the Internet makes it easier for individuals to get hold of information. They can pull down the information they want irrespective of where they are in the world. Before the Internet, one woman in an Indian village would have had great difficulty accessing information from the US Navy.

In the last chapter, we suggested that a networked society could promote sustainable development as ICT creates the scale and feedback mechanisms to make empathy a force for change. This relies on access to information. Information creates the feedback that promotes empathy in the networked system and it equips individuals to respond. In this kind of system, access to so much information is a real opportunity. But there's a risk that individuals will be overwhelmed. Empowering people depends on using ICT as a pull rather than a push medium, and on organizations opening up so that individuals can find the information they're looking for.

Creating for inclusion

Ohmynews[2] is an online newspaper from South Korea. What's different about it is that the general public writes it. Teacher, housewife or journalist – it doesn't really matter. As long as you have a story to tell and can get it down in writing, the paper will publish your work. The few employed journalists (by training) only edit for language and factual accuracy. 'The main concept is that every citizen can be a reporter. We changed the concept of the reporter', said the editor Oh Yeon-ho.[3] The newspaper has been running for three years and has become so popular that, after winning the presidential election in February 2003, the new South Korean president gave his first interview to Ohmynews.

Professor of regional economic development, Richard Florida, has observed the rise of a new type of worker whose function it is to create new ideas, new technologies and new creative content. Florida calls this new breed the 'creative class'. But examples such as Ohmynews challenge the idea that creativity is the preserve of the few in the digital society. On the contrary, it appears that ICT is leading to the democratization of creativity, or 'mass amateurization' as technology commentator Clay Shirky has described it. The number of blogs has exploded with new ones being set up every minute, and in Denmark one in five adults has been involved in building a website. The Internet is a free, global space, a 'creative commons' where any creation can find an audience anywhere in the world at almost no cost.[4]

This is a dramatic change from the offline world. The reality of hard copy publishing can be tough. Even a runaway success such as JK Rowling's *Harry Potter* series can be rejected several times before being published. The costs of production and distribution make the barriers to entry high and give people with links to commercial publishers an advantage. In contrast, it costs only £30 to register a domain name and set up a blog and the software for this is free to download. In the world of music, wannabe pop stars no longer need a state of the art studio and expensive equipment to make a recording. A home computer, a microphone and the right software will do. The opportunity for individuals to create their own content could be a powerful driver for a more diverse and inclusive society.

Self-expression through creativity fulfils a basic human need and can play an important part in social inclusion. The aim of the story-telling site ABCTales.com is to showcase writing talent and provide opportunities for creativity. In June 2003, the site featured over 29,000 different stories from thousands of different authors. The website tells us that: 'An outreach team of 'tale-catchers' tours the country encouraging people – including prisoners, homeless people, refugees and the elderly – to tell their stories and join the ABCtales community of readers and writers'.

Content creation can also be an important way to reintegrate people into a learning environment, moving them up the digital ladder. Combining creative content with technology can be a productive mix. For individuals with limited literacy, multimedia content, combining pictures and sound, can break down the barriers to learning characteristic of word-based materials and methods. At the same time, people develop valuable skills for today's economy: creativity, content development and digital literacy.

Alongside benefits for individuals, digital content can offer a lifeline to communities. For many years, the United Nations Educational, Scientific and Cultural Organization (UNESCO) has painstakingly collected samples of indigenous music as a historical record of the world's cultures. The Internet can do this and more, by providing a forum for active expression of different cultures. Professor of linguistics David Crystal certainly thinks that the Internet could be a powerful tool for cultural preservation. 'The Internet has a glorious multilingual future ahead of it. It does in fact offer an opportunity for all languages to have a global presence, and this is especially important for minority and endangered languages… Before the Internet, the chances of a minority language bringing its concerns in front of a world audience were minimal. Now it's routine.'[5]

Professor Crystal is quick to remind us that we're still talking about potential in many parts of the world. He gives the example of a popular computer centre in Johannesburg in South Africa. The centre has twelve computers but there's only enough electricity to power up two at a time. This means that people wait in queues outside, while computers stand idle inside.

We face tremendous barriers to giving everyone access to the network. Poorer regions don't yet have reliable electricity supplies let alone Internet access. But there is an opportunity to use relevant content to make the digital society reflect the full diversity of human life.

RT Mark and the Decepticons

Margaret is a pensioner living in a council block in Westminster in London run by the housing organization, Integer. Margaret's block is different from the surrounding ones because it's fitted with the latest IT systems. For example, Integer has installed a system that monitors utilities in the building. This allows the company to manage the environmental impact of the building and helps Margaret keep an eye on how much she spends on electricity, gas and water each week. This information makes all the difference to Margaret's quality of life. It gives her better control over her money, making her small pension stretch that bit further.

Access to information allows individuals more control over the decisions they make. *The Cluetrain Manifesto*, one of the most influential books about how the Internet is changing business, argued that widespread access to information is giving civil society greater control over corporations.[6] The same process of empowerment we see at the individual level is happening in society.

The Internet opens a door into the inner workings of business and gives users unprecedented access to information about companies, their activities and their effects on a global scale. Most companies have websites containing information that was available before the Internet but much less accessible. Annual reports are available to download, and typically press releases, financial statements, the names and even the contact details of key staff are also easily accessed. In today's digital society, even information that companies try to hide somehow finds its way out.

Political and environmental activists are getting better and better at using electronic networks to coordinate global campaigns, bringing a wider constituency of protest to bear on perceived wrongdoers. What makes these networks particularly powerful is their ability to exploit information to keep pressure up on companies to improve their social and environmental perform-ance. Former Chief Economist at the OECD and arch-critic of corporate responsibility, David Henderson, argues that the Internet has caused a step-change in the ability of non-governmental organizations (NGOs) to organize and mount effective campaigns against businesses, and has been one of the primary causes of the rise of CSR.[7]

Websites have been set up to target particular companies or malpractice, presenting information on activities that would have struggled to see the light of day before the Internet became a tool of popular communication. Shell has been a victim of the activist group RTMark (now archived at www.rtmark. com/shell) while, during the controversy over genetically modified crops, Monsanto fell foul of a cyber activist group called the Decepticons who set up www.monsantos.org. Protest using the Internet has grown in sophistication, as activists have learned the skills of computer hackers[8] to assault and harry companies through their websites, or even disrupt internal web-based systems, in a phenomenon referred to as 'hacktivism'. One way of thinking of hacktivism is as an online version of civil disobedience, or 'Electronic Civil Disobedience' (a term initially coined by the Critical Art Ensemble). Virtual blockades and virtual sit-ins can be thought of as the equivalents of physical blockades and trespass.

It's not just NGOs and hacktivists who are using the networks to exchange information in protest. As the world was preparing for war in Iraq in 2003, with or without a final resolution from the UN, anti-war petitions were bouncing their way around the globe. Emails with lists of people objecting to the war arrived on desktops and laptops, with instructions to forward to the White House. Text messages were circulated from mobile to mobile, with instructions of numbers to ring to register protest and to forward the text message to all the names stored on the phone. These kinds of activities could be dismissed as worthy but ineffectual. But as mass spontaneous protest over electronic networks grows in scale and sophistication, and as online protest joins with protest in the street, it will become more effective at holding those in power to account.

The corporate response

In response to pressure for greater transparency and accountability, com-panies wishing to get ahead are seeking to make more information available about their environmental and social impacts. ICT provides new tools for companies to do this and helps them in managing how this information is collected and disseminated. Our research for Digital Europe revealed that today's extended supply chains could be an impediment to greater social responsibility. But using ICT to effectively manage information coming from different suppliers can provide a solution.

To understand the environmental impacts of a product or service requires a lot of time spent gathering complex sets of data and crunching numbers. The challenge is nowhere more acute than in the ICT sector. With technology evolving rapidly and pressure to increase the speed with which new products are delivered to market, environmental impact assessments are often the first thing out of the window. What's more, the source of ingredients in the recipe for the same product can change on a daily basis, even within the same company, depending on what is available and how much it costs. Take two laptop computers apart, one produced a week after the other, and the components inside could be sourced from entirely different places, as the Wuppertal Institute discovered in their research with HP.[9]

HP is a company that takes its responsibility to society seriously. The company has a statement of corporate values and one of its business principles, 'global citizenship', underpins its approach to managing the social and environmental impacts of its operations. The governance structure gives high priority to corporate responsibility, with a board-level representative reporting directly to the Chief Executive. The Wuppertal Institute's work with HP concentrated on comparing the environmental impacts of a couple of its products, a handheld computer and a laptop computer that delivered similar functions. The Wuppertal Institute uses a MIPS methodology for making these kinds of calculations. MIPS stands for 'material input per service unit', and involves collecting detailed information on all the materials required for the end product: all the raw materials used in manufacture, the energy used, the transport requirements, everything right down to the cardboard boxes and packaging that components arrive in.

From the start of the handheld/laptop analysis, it became clear that it was going to be a struggle to get all the information from HP's suppliers that was needed. The computers being analysed were complex pieces of machinery, made up of a large number of separate components from different suppliers in different locations around the world. Many of the suppliers when contacted couldn't provide the level of detail required for the calculations. This meant that the Wuppertal Institute had to literally take apart the devices they were testing, weigh each component and estimate its composition. Having a flexible network of interchangeable suppliers makes it difficult to know what is in a final product and consequently it's very difficult to make steady improvements in the product's sustainability impacts.

Turn the situation on its head, and the global reach and complex interconnections of the supply network could work in favour of sustainable development if used to share information between suppliers. It's difficult for any one company to single-handedly monitor environmental and social impacts throughout its entire supply chain. If all companies involved in the network filed social and environmental data about components electronically, companies would have access to information coming from the entire network. This kind of system could only work with widespread buy-in across markets, but pressure from leading companies like HP could help persuade reluctant suppliers to come on board. The network could be linked to existing schemes such as the Life Cycle Assessment initiative of the United Nations Environment Programme.

Other sectors face similar challenges. As more sectors build ICT into their business models, the boundaries between one sector and another become blurred, reducing the influence of any one player over the value chain. Who's to blame if a computer crashes halfway through a banking transaction: the bank, the software design company, the Internet service provider, the hardware supplier or all four? In such an environment, the importance of cross-sector cooperation to address social and environmental impacts is vital. Product or service panels that bring together the different companies in the chain will be an essential feature of leadership on supply chain issues. In such cases, ICT provides important tools for collecting, collating and sharing information.

Once it is collected, environmental and social information needs to be effectively communicated to stakeholders. In the Digital Europe survey, we asked CSR practitioners about the use of ICT in communicating with different groups. Figure 4.1 shows that ebusiness applications were being used most with employees or customers. Of the companies where ICT was used a great deal or fair amount for communicating with stakeholders, almost half said that it had significantly increased the quality of communication, with another 20 per cent saying ICT had slightly increased the quality of communication. This could be because the information was more targeted, more effectively communicated or simply because there was more of it – use of ICT can help with all of these.[10]

In a series of follow up interviews, we were able to find out more about how ICT is improving communication within companies by increasing access to information. The people we spoke to generally felt that easier access to company information gave employees a better understanding of strategy and made them more comfortable engaging with management. Company intranets were particularly important for this. By allowing previously inaccessible information to flow with relative freedom to all members of the organization, intranets created a sense of openness and unity, helping new recruits to integrate and building more cohesive teams.

Evidence suggests that online reporting reaches a greater number of people

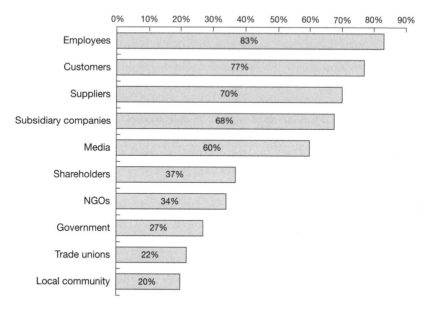

Figure 4.1 *Virtual communication with stakeholders: 'To what extent would you say ebusiness is used in your company's communication with the following stakeholder groups?' (Per cent A great deal / A fair amount, Base: 100 companies)*
Source: MORI and Forum for the Future

than printed reports – HP reports an impressive 13,000 downloads of its environmental and social report a month. But few companies make use of the possibilities of providing real time information and encouraging feedback on social and environmental issues. Regular reporting cycles are important for benchmarking performance, but more real time information could be a valuable complement. BT reports on its sustainability performance almost exclusively online and is therefore able to provide frequent updates to its content. The website also provides opportunities for visitors to give feedback, through online debates or feedback forms, so that the CSR team can respond to this feedback on a continual basis. The technology exists to make CSR websites genuinely interactive forums for regular communication between companies and stakeholders. At the moment, this kind of approach is disappointingly rare.

In his contribution in box 4.1, Sean Gilbert of the Global Reporting

Initiative explains how the development of a common framework for corporate sustainability reporting can guide the social and environmental performance of business.

Box 4.1 *A compass for ICT*
Sean Gilbert

ICT undeniably creates new forms of value for society and will be an important part of pursuing sustainable development. Our ability to benefit from this will rely on developing tools to help us assess and optimize the nature of the value created for as wide a range of stakeholders as possible.

The simple existence of technology does not guarantee that everyone will have equal access to it, or have the same ability to enjoy the benefits that it can offer. We must make sound choices in deciding where to invest our research and development energies – not all technologies offer equal added value for sustainable development. Technology brings changes to consumption and production patterns and, while clearly offering improvements in some areas, the net change may be for the worse.

The industry itself plays the lead role in marshalling and applying the resources necessary to innovate and deliver ICT products and services. Its business models and interpretations of signals from the marketplace have a direct impact on the nature and distribution of ICT products. Industry activities clearly respond to the market environment, but also have an impact on it. For this reason, reporting at the corporate level is essential to help us understand the type of value being created by ICT and how this value is added.

The Global Reporting Initiative (GRI) has been developing a framework for sustainability reporting through a multi-stakeholder process since 1997 and its *Sustainability Reporting Guidelines* have now been used by over 200 major organizations.[11] It has recently begun the development of sectoral supplements, including one for telecoms. The emergence of the GRI and its recognition by leaders from business, trade unions, civil society and the investment community is a sign of the widespread desire for a generally accepted framework for organizational reporting.

Perhaps the most challenging and essential part of this process relates to product impacts. The reporting of internal operations is relatively well-trodden ground and approaches to measuring on-site environmental and social performance are increasingly well understood and accepted. Measuring performance in supply-chains raises questions of logistics and relative responsibilities, but again can be understood based on existing practices. Product impacts enter into a much more complex area, since this information is not easily accessible and isolating the impacts that result directly from the use of a product is difficult. But it is this information that is most important in understanding how an individual company's decisions are contributing to sustainable development.

The need to understand product impacts underlines the importance of ensuring that corporate-level reporting can be related to other types of indicators such as national or regional performance indicators. Enabling effective public–private partnerships and coordination relies on being able to look at the performance of an individual organization in the context of other objectives. Similarly, assessing product impacts requires an understanding of the external context in which a company is operating.

Choosing and implementing measures of corporate performance will inevitably raise questions about the relative responsibilities of government, industry and the consumer. Reporting is a platform upon which such exchanges can take place, goals can be agreed and accountability delivered. This understanding of responsibilities will evolve over time, but a robust practice of reporting can help direct it. It could act as a compass for ICT and sustainable development.

Governments can play an enabling role by guaranteeing stakeholders a certain baseline for environmental and social reporting. Governments in Denmark, France and the Netherlands have done this by making it mandatory for certain companies to report on their sustainability as well as financial performance. A set of standard sustainability indicators gives the stakeholders confidence in the quality of the information they receive. The European Commission and governments in EU countries could build on this initiative and move to mandatory reporting across the EU. Similarly, standard use of a small set of sustainability indicators online would make information on the web more credible and facilitate comparison between companies. A CSR portal on the Internet, collecting information from across different sectors, seems like an obvious next step and could have the effect of shaming poorly performing companies into action.

Information glut

In 1999 only 35 per cent of the Global Fortune Top 250 produced an environmental, social or sustainability report in addition to their financial report. By 2002, 45 per cent were doing so. But Jonathon Porritt and journalist Roger Cowe maintain that much reporting continues to be superficial –

quantity not quality. Of the top 250 UK quoted companies, 159 made some public disclosure about their sustainability activities in 2001, but only 36 had the information externally verified. In the same year, 79 of the top 100 quoted companies in the UK published some information on their social impacts but only a quarter included any quantitative data.[12]

Findings from the Digital Europe survey suggested that the use of ICT to communicate with stakeholders was more pronounced where communication takes place on a regular basis, for example with customers and employees, and involves a large number of people with a variety of different information needs. Here, the tendency may be for companies to use ICT to push large volumes of information out, safe in the knowledge that people will be able to find what they want if they look long and hard enough.

Communication with trades unions, investors or government officials is less frequent and companies adopt a more personal, targeted strategy, in which a push approach to information release is thought to be less effective. The survey findings suggest that companies responding to calls for greater transparency and accountability are often simply adding to the information glut.

It is now 2 million times cheaper to store information digitally than it was 50 years ago, and we are storing more of it than ever before. There is a fine line between abundant information and information overload. Overstepping the line can lead to disempowerment as we become overwhelmed by the cacophony around us.

A global survey of 1,000 business managers found that the surfeit of technology-generated information made more than 60 per cent of them tense and stressed.[13] The need to keep up to date encourages overwork but does not always pay dividends. The human capacity to filter and process information is not infinite. Psychologists are reporting signs of information fatigue syndrome, leading to reduced concentration, disturbed sleep and even immune deficiency.

Many office workers experience this on a daily basis, just by returning to their desks after lunch or a meeting to be faced with dozens of new emails. Unsolicited junk email – or spam – is a major culprit of information overload. As part of an investigation into spam, the US Federal Trade Commission created email addresses and posted them in chat rooms and newsgroups. It took just nine minutes for the first spam email to be received. In 2003, anti-spam services reported more than 5 million unique spam attacks a month, three times more than in 2002.[14] While researching for Digital Europe, we spoke to managers who complained of a drop in the productivity of their staff because of the time spent dealing with email. One interviewee even claimed that 'email is killing us'.

It's useful to distinguish between information overload and interaction overload. Think about mobile phones. How many of us have changed our behaviour since getting a mobile? We now call from the bus to say we'll be five minutes late or from the supermarket to confirm the evening's menu. This can strengthen relationships, prevent isolation and also increase personal safety. But this change in behaviour can as easily lead to interaction overload. Even though we adapt and find ways of coping with increased interaction, for many it is still a source of stress and tension. In the case of email both information and interaction overload can be a problem, but it's the need to respond that causes most stress.

With ICT we're interacting more, but has the quality of interaction actually improved? That's surely a more significant question. Colleagues who used to walk across the office to speak to each other now email from their seats. A study by America's Northwestern University found that business negotiations conducted electronically ran into more difficulties than those that began with a getting-to-know-you phone chat.[15] In his recent pamphlet, 'Heidegger, Habermas and the Mobile Phone', George Myerson of King's College, London argued that much of the interaction that mobiles support is more akin to consumption than communication. He says of text messages: 'to make such messages definitive for mainstream communication is to exclude most of the possibilities of human expression. It's a black and white universe.'[16]

But David Crystal argues that the increased range of communication media available today shouldn't be seen as a threat. He says that ICT, like previous technologies, is making language 'stylistically richer: 'Printing brought a huge range of new graphic conventions and varieties. And it is the same with the language associated with the new technologies. These don't affect the rest of the language, which continues to develop and change regardless. The whole point is that these new uses are technology-related, so there is no real way in which they could seriously affect the rest of the language. I am not going to start text-abbreviating in my general usage just because I can do it on a mobile phone.'[17]

With any new technology, there's always controversy over the scope and nature of its social impacts and a period of adjustment where disruption is particularly acute. Over time, we learn to integrate the technology more effectively into social interactions. Technology itself can help us manage information, and technology etiquette can alleviate the problem to some extent (for example specifying in the subject heading whether an email requires action or is only for information). However, a more effective solution is for organizations – companies, governments and civil society groups – to recognize the Internet as a pull not a push medium and open themselves up to allow people to find the information they want.

Open policy

Go to Ecover.com and you can find out how Ecover makes its environmentally friendly cleaning products. If you're a chemist you can go away and make them yourself. The company actively invites you to steal its formula, recognizing that by giving other people this information, it's contributing to its mission to promote sustainable development. Ecover is breaking the corporate mould with its open approach to information and communication.

Ecover's approach shouldn't be dismissed just because it's a small, values-driven company set up explicitly to aid the environment. Other organizations should embrace their approach if we're going to make information on the network a driver for sustainable development. People need to be empowered to make decisions in the interests of sustainable development and this depends on their being able to pull down from the network relevant information rather than being overwhelmed by information being pushed at them. The Internet makes this technically possible. But it can only work if companies and governments open themselves up to stakeholders and use the Internet to allow people to find the information they want.

It needn't be a one-way deal. ICT gives governments and companies the opportunity to use the creativity of the entire network to tackle their sustainability challenges. In a Forum for the Future pamphlet, *Open Policy*, Paul Miller explains how the idea could work:

> *'Organizations would set the criteria for a particular policy (say, cutting their carbon dioxide emissions by 20 per cent by 2010), but then would open up the decision to anyone who might wish to contribute. Using the web, they would provide all the information available to contributors who would then be able to post ideas as to how the goals could be met. A system [...] where users rate the postings of other users for usefulness and relevance would ensure the best ideas gradually move up the agenda.'*[18]

Open policy uses the connectivity of the network and the power of information in the interests of sustainable development. Crucially it depends on companies opening up to stakeholders. In this way, people can be empowered by information rather than overwhelmed by it.

But in an information-rich environment, there is still the problem of misinformation. People need some way of sorting the wheat from the chaff – they need to know where to pull information down from. This is where trust comes in. In the next chapter we explore how trust allows us to sort through the information on the network and the information we receive from other people. Trust is our guide in the digital society.

WEBS OF TRUST

The European youth summit held in Brussels in 2002 was all about corporate responsibility. In one of the sessions, participants were asked to raise their hands if they trusted business. A surprising number did so. When asked their reasons, they said that 'we trust them, but we trust them to behave badly'. 48 per cent of the 34,000 people surveyed by the World Economic Forum (WEF) in 2003 said that they had little or no trust in global companies to operate in society's best interest and only 33 per cent had some or a lot of trust in global company executives.[1]

Greater consumer choice makes trust harder to build and more easily lost. Advertising campaigns and special offers are constantly encouraging us to switch electricity providers, change banks or try a different brand of washing powder. If one brand loses our trust, we try another. It's a difficult environment for maintaining trust and that makes trust a hot commodity for business. Management consultants Ciancutti and Steding explain that: 'Trust is more than a highly esteemed value. Along with technology and innovation, it is one of the most powerful forces driving business today. We are a society in search of Trust. The less we find it, the more precious it becomes. An organization in which people earn one another's trust and that commands trust from the public, has a competitive advantage. It can draw the best people, inspire consumer loyalty, reach out successfully to new markets and provide more innovative products and services.'[2]

Business is not the lone target of public mistrust. Trust in traditional institutions and figures of authority is also in decline. In the same WEF survey, just over half the respondents reported having little or no trust in national parliaments and 42 per cent said that their trust in government leaders had declined since 2001.[3] The reasons behind this are intricate and involved, associated with grand processes of social transformation and economic restructuring. What's relevant for us is the fundamental role that increasing access to information through ICT has played in this process.

Government and business have attempted to build trust with greater transparency and availability of information. In the first of the 2002 BBC Reith lectures on the philosophy of trust, Onora O'Neill, professor of philosophy at Cambridge University, challenged the assumption that more information is somehow automatically good for trust. 'How can we tell which claims and counterclaims, reports and supposed facts are trustworthy, when so much information swirls round us?' she asked. 'It is hard to distinguish rumour from report, fact from fiction, reliable source from disinformant, truth-teller from deceiver... It is quite clear that the very technologies that spread information so easily and efficiently, are every bit as good at spreading misinformation and disinformation.'[4]

Too much information can actually undermine trust. It becomes easier to call into question traditionally held views and trusted positions in society. For instance, patients often turn up to hospital or their doctor's surgery with pages of printed information from the Internet, prepared to challenge the doctor's opinion based on their own online research. It's a positive development that more people are taking greater interest in their health and actively seeking information, but if this leads to patients ignoring medical advice because 'the Internet told them what was wrong with them', it could be an unhealthy development.

The erosion of trust poses a serious dilemma in an information-rich society. Whether it's information flowing on the network, such as content on websites, or information we receive directly from other people, trust allows us to sort through it all and identify what's relevant to us. We need trust to operate in both contexts. Online, we need ways of identifying trustworthy sources from the wealth of possible choices and, in wider society, we need trust to facilitate the exchange of information between people.

In this chapter we look at whether trust between people and trust in information can be built in cyberspace. We argue that the online environment is not rich in trust, but this doesn't mean that ICT inevitably erodes trust. In the context of existing social networks where there is already some trust, ICT can help build the trust between people that facilitates the flow of useful information.

Trusted sources

Of regular Internet users, half are unwilling to engage in commercial transactions online because they lack trust in the ability of websites to protect their personal information.[5] Trust has always been a problem for Internet users: how do you know that people are who they say they are online? How do you know that what you read is accurate? In the physical world, there are ultimately no guarantees either. But we rely on social clues to guide us to trusted sources. For example, we use eye contact or tone of voice to decide whether someone is trustworthy or should be avoided. It's no accident that banks used to be palatial, solid buildings. It was an unspoken way of impressing on customers their trustworthiness and reliability.

It's not surprising, therefore, that when the Internet started to become popular, the most visited websites quickly became those with links to already trusted sources. The most popular websites for news tend to be the online arms of established offline players, such as the BBC and CNN. Similarly, when ecommerce was just taking off, high street brand strength carried over to the Internet and ensured that 'clicks and mortar' ecommerce websites became more successful than the agile Internet start-ups they emulated. Eight out of the ten biggest online banks in the UK are simply the online versions of established high street banks, such as Barclays or NatWest.[6]

All very well if you have an offline brand to leverage, but what if you don't? Many websites have in-built reputation systems that try to build trust with their users. For example, regular visitors to Amazon are greeted on the homepage with recommendations, books that people with a similar purchasing history have also bought. The search engine Google also runs an automated reputation system, listing at the top of the page those web pages that have the most links to other websites. Not all reputation systems work behind the scenes like this. Amazon refines its automated system by allowing users to score the books they have already read. eBay, the online auction site, asks buyers and sellers to rate the trustworthiness of the people they are buying and selling from.

Other systems try to build trust by restricting users to certain parts of the Internet, recognizing that its sheer size and diversity can be bewildering. One example is the Cybrarian project, run by the Department for Education and Skills in the UK. It aims to develop a web portal that will act as a trusted intermediary, getting people online by leading them to the most relevant content, simplifying web pages and providing guidance on how to use and make the best of different sites. Estimates indicate that as much as 40 per cent of the UK population lacks the literacy, cognitive or physical skills to make full use of the Internet without some help and guidance.[7] For these people, Cybrarian could be the tool that gets them off the bottom rung of the digital ladder.

Certain commercial Internet service providers (ISPs), for example AOL, create their own world of content. These webs within the web are referred to as 'walled gardens'. They allow ISPs to tailor content specifically to their users, encouraging them to stay within a safe environment rather than roaming the wider Internet.

But there's an inherent risk in any approach that restricts exposure to diversity of content and opinion. For example, Usenet, the Internet-based network of newsgroups and discussion forums, includes a feature called 'Killfile' that can be used to screen out offensive language, disagreeable opinions, the contributions of certain disliked people or even whole topics of conversation. This results in a more welcoming and trustworthy environment for discussion, but less exposure to a variety of information sources. Cass Sunstein, professor of law at the University of Chicago, worries about the wider social effects of people sealing themselves off entirely from different views and interests online, in what he calls 'echo chambers'. Sunstein reminds us of the value of difference of opinion: 'it is important to realize that a well-functioning democracy depends not just on freedom from censorship, but also on a set of common experiences and on unsought, unanticipated and even unwanted exposures to diverse topics, people and ideas'.[8]

An increase in choice makes it easier for people to exist in silos, surrounded by others with similar backgrounds, lifestyles and opinions. These echo chambers help us identify trusted sources of information, but can have the perverse effect of undermining trust between people. Exposure to shared ideas and diversity of opinions is an important part of building generalized trust in wider society – how likely people are to trust a stranger.

This is where the open policy approach to information and communications we discussed in the last chapter comes in. In 2002 the Cooperative Bank came top of the pile in the UK for sustainability reporting.[9] Meanwhile, in research conducted by the New Economics Foundation, the company was voted the most trusted in the UK.[10] Companies that leave trust in the hands of marketeers and brand managers might be missing a trick. Organizations that adopt an open approach to communications, covering the full range of their impacts on society, and use the Internet to allow people to pull down the information they want, can build trust with stakeholders: trust in the information the company provides and trust in the company itself.

Trusted networks

When the Internet was first developed, it was used primarily by a relatively small band of technologists, many with a common interest in improving the software that made the Internet work. Now, it's host to a bewildering variety of different communities of interest. There are forums for all sorts of specialized fields, from fans of the Grateful Dead to speakers of minority languages and people trying to give up smoking. It's probably fair to say that the variety of special interest groups online mirrors the variety of those groups in the offline world. And these online forums can be useful in providing support and information. Take the medical profession as an example. Doctors around the world faced with a medical mystery can log on to the web and share their queries with others in the field. Medicine has a long tradition of knowledge sharing anyway, but before the Internet it took place through conferences, journals and telephone calls. The web has made it possible to seriously improve that knowledge sharing: information is always accessible and answers to questions can come back almost instantly, from a vast number of people.

This kind of virtual knowledge sharing is also increasingly vital within multinational companies, where peers work on similar issues thousands of miles apart. For example, sustainability professionals working for HP across the world use the company's greenbase website to collate and share environmental feedback from customers. BP's personal development programme, 'Learning to Fly', allows employees anywhere in the world facing similar professional challenges to make contact with each other to share knowledge and ideas.

Virtual communities like these emerged at a time when academics, politicians and the media were growing increasingly worried about the demise of communities based around traditional institutions, such as the church or local neighbourhood. People looked to virtual communities to provide a way of generating trust and wider social value just as local community had done at the beginning of the twentieth century.

In 1916 a West Virginia school superintendent called Lyda Judson Hanifan noted that high levels of participation among local people in school affairs not only led to improved support for the school, but also to general improvements in the wider community. To explain why this might be, he coined the term 'social capital'. We've talked about one aspect of social capital already – networks. Trust is another. Robert Putnam, one of the world's leading thinkers on social capital, defines it as: 'features of social life – networks, norms and trust – that enable participants to act together more effectively to pursue shared objectives'.[11]

Trust is often used as an indicator of social capital and, like social capital, high levels of trust are associated with positive social and economic outcomes, although social capital theorists are quick to remind us that negative outcomes are also possible. What is the wider value of trust?

The world values survey, run by the University of Michigan in the US, measures levels of generalized trust in a selection of different countries by asking: 'Generally speaking, would you say that most people can be trusted or that you cannot be too careful in dealing with people?'. The results of the survey show that trust levels vary widely from country to country. For example, Norway scored highest in 1996 with 65 per cent of people saying that they trusted others. The lowest scoring country was Brazil, with only 3 per cent. There's a strong correlation on a country-by-country basis between levels of GDP per capita and trust: higher trust countries tend to be more economically prosperous.

This isn't just theory. According to Paul Zak of Claremount Graduate University: 'Trust is among the most powerful stimulants for investment and economic growth that economists have discovered' – largely through its role in underwriting investments.[12] Where trust is high, investments are cheaper, as the parties involved don't have to spend money on extra security.

The importance of trust doesn't end there. Paul Zak and colleague Ahlam Fakhar analysed the links between trust and 85 different social, economic and environmental indicators. They found that high levels of trust are associated with a bizarre range of different factors, from breastfeeding, sexual activity and consumption of vegetables, to levels of education, rule of law and strong institutions. Low levels of trust correlated with political instability and poor water and air quality.[13]

Their findings echo the conclusions of a recent discussion paper from the UK government entitled 'Why is social capital important?'. It identified six general social and economic benefits:[14]

1 It may facilitate higher levels of GDP.
2 It may facilitate the more efficient functioning of job markets.
3 It may facilitate educational attainment.
4 It may contribute to lower levels of crime.
5 It may lead to better health.
6 It may improve the effectiveness of institutions of government.

Trust helps to secure the exchange of information between different parts of the social network, a process that underpins many of the positive social and economic outcomes it's associated with.

For the most part, trust and social capital get built through face-to-face interaction between people on the street, at work, in cafes and so on. Nowadays, an increasing amount of interaction takes place virtually – nothing new, of course: an old fashioned, handwritten letter is an example of virtual communication. But with the Internet, it has become possible to emulate 'real' community, because the Internet supports so many different types of interaction, from emails between two people, to vast many-to-many exchanges such as newsgroups or discussion boards. But is it possible in these purely virtual communities to build the levels of trust that encourage people to share information and trust the information they receive from others?

According to Clay Shirky, to provide social value an online community needs to be like a ship. It needs to have a direction and it needs to have a limited number of passengers. This is where purely virtual communities have tended to come unstuck. They often grow too big and become dominated by a few players with the rest acting as their audience, rather than being a group where everyone has a certain responsibility to participate. If the group is so large that most of the members don't know each other, it becomes difficult to build trust and maintain a sense of belonging.[15] Without this, the community can't support discussion or differences of opinion and its purpose becomes reduced to a lowest common denominator view. You either support AC Milan or you don't. You are either against the building of a motorway through your village or you aren't.

The failings of purely virtual communities say more about the way that trust is built between people than the limited potential of ICT to contribute to social capital. Tim Berners-Lee, creator of the worldwide web, recognized that the web was not a parallel space but existed in a social context: 'Take a book as an example' he said. 'You read it because it was referred to you by a reliable source. In the same way somebody you know may point to a web site. Trust is always transferred from one individual to another.'[16]

Electronic networks are most powerful when embedded into existing social networks, where the trust needed for information to flow already exists and can be built on. As ICT becomes an everyday part of people's lives, there's a clear trend towards a closer connection between virtual community and real world community. ICT is being used to build trust by augmenting real world interaction, unleashing the potential of information on the network to empower individual choices and action.

This is where Paul Resnick at Michigan University sees the real value in the relationship between ICT and social capital: making new forms of interaction possible. Although activity using ICT can be less immersive and more impersonal than traditional social relations, it's still valuable.[17] He gives the example of neighbourhood email lists that may lie dormant for months, but can easily be revived to inform residents of a recent burglary. Look at activity on the email list alone and you may get an impression of an inactive community. But look at the email list and all the other local activities together and you start getting a better impression of the community's health. And this healthy level of trust within the community makes the email list an effective means of sharing information among residents when it's used. In his comment in box 5.1, Resnick explores this observation in more depth.

There have been many attempts to use ICT to improve existing community. The website www.dansk-i-sydslesvig.de is a popular community website for the Danish community in Germany. Numerous battles and disputes over the drawing of the border between Denmark and Germany have left a Danish minority on the German side of the border and, as you would expect, it's very protective of its language and culture. The website tells users how to find a Danish speaking doctor or lawyer, which schools teach Danish and how to get Danish radio and TV in Germany. It's a community hub and plays a

Box 5.1 *Where locality meets virtuality*
Paul Resnick

Technology has created new ways for people to make and maintain social connections. People can communicate at a distance and exchange messages asynchronously or quickly catch up on missed conversations. They can maintain weak or latent ties, to be activated when needed.

Whenever a new way of accomplishing some 'function' emerges, observers tend to notice first a substitution effect of the new for the old. Then there is what economists call an income effect, an increase in how much the function is performed overall. Finally, new structures emerge that rely on cheap ubiquitous availability of that function. This was the case for transport, as railways and then automobiles replaced the horse-drawn carriage.[18] It's now also the case with computer mediated communication.

We can make plausible speculations about what some of the new structures in this final phase might look like. These structures will mix the physical and virtual, using geographic proximity to organize virtual interaction and technology to mediate activity in physical space. Consider some examples of each.

First, geography has become a natural and widespread basis for matching people to content and conversations. UpMyStreet.com invites users to enter the postal code where they live or want to make connections. The site then displays local information (schools, cafes, etc.) and also shows the messages contributed by people who live closest to that postal code. The system scales well as more users participate: with few users, readers see messages from people perhaps 100km away; with more users, they make connections in their neighbourhood.

An even more interesting hybrid of the physical and virtual exists in the community of adventurers that has emerged around the site geocaching.com. Someone places a physical cache containing a few interesting curiosities (playing cards, for example) in a hidden location, then posts the global positioning system (GPS) coordinates of the cache on the website. When another adventurer finds the cache, he takes something from it and leaves something else in its place, so the contents of the cache evolve. He then leaves a comment on the website, creating a connection over time among the people who have found the cache. According to the site there are now caches hidden in 171 countries.

It can also work the other way around, with virtuality seeping into physical interactions. In neighbourhoods, researchers have explored the effects of photo directories and email lists.[19] At meetings, researchers have experimented with small, wearable electronic devices known as meme tags. These alert the wearer whenever someone wearing a compatible tag passes nearby. One can imagine similar technology seeping into all sorts of every day scenarios. For example, airlines might offer to automatically seat people near compatible fellow travellers, grouping the tennis fans together or perhaps merely the people interested in conversation rather than sleep.

Perhaps a mix of physical and virtual can even help to overhaul transportation systems, enabling a hybrid between notions of public and private. Hitchhiking has declined drastically in the US in the past half century, but in a few metropolitan areas, it has emerged in a new form. Drivers pick up riders at suburban locations in order to fill up their cars, making them eligible to use less congested 'high occupancy vehicle' lanes. Conventions have developed for where to wait in line, depending on one's destination. Now imagine how this institution might evolve if participants used cell phones and websites to coordinate ride matching. A reputation system might help people weed out bad matches ('Previous riders reported that this driver drove too fast') and ease safety fears, since ride matches would be registered and thus an abductor could be traced. The meme tag idea might even make such ride matching more fun: drivers and passengers might be alerted when they had mutual acquaintances in common, or graduated from the same secondary school or university, without revealing this information to those without matching characteristics.

There has been a decline in traditional ways of connecting, and thus a decline in valuable social capital, at least in the US where Robert Putnam described the symptomatic phenomenon of declining local bowling leagues.[20] It is an open question whether virtual ties can adequately substitute as a generator of social capital. But a focus merely on substitution effects may obscure the more important trends and opportunities. The income effect suggests that there will be more social interaction overall. Most importantly, new forms of social relations are emerging that could not exist without combining locality and virtuality. It is there that we should look for the emergence of socio-technical capital to substitute for declining participation in bowling leagues.[21]

supporting role in keeping the community of Danish speakers together, preserving their language and culture.

The success of that website is based on the shared experiences of its users as a small minority in a large country. Lordshiplane.co.uk is a website serving the community in one small area of south London. Here are some short excerpts from one of its discussion boards:

- 'HELLO EVERYONE! I was wondering if any of you could please tell me if you have heard of a Goodrich road school. I'm doing some family tracing and I have just found out that my nan went to this school… please, please any info would help as I'm desperate to find my family: surname GWYNN'

- 'Is anyone else fed up with people parking in the mother and baby parking spaces when they do not have children with them? – New mum'

- 'I'm new to the area and would like to know if anyone can recommend: 1) a good builder as I have some minor frost damage to the front bay of my property; 2) a good dentist – one that's not a butcher or a preacher! Thanks – Jason'

Although these three people aren't necessarily representative of all of the site's users, their contributions illustrate how their common connection to a certain place facilitates the sharing of relevant information. The space on the Internet is a bit like another pavement, marketplace or post office noticeboard.

This facility isn't limited to the Internet. Entrepreneur Paul Kent has set up a service called Community Alerts.[22] The idea is to collect a database of people registering to receive text alerts on their mobiles about local events and services, such as reports of bogus callers in the area, electricity cuts or changes to dustbin collection times. Crucially, users only receive the type of texts they have registered for, and the system won't be used for sales or promotions. With this system in place, communities could respond much more quickly to local emergencies. If a child is reported missing, for example, text messages can be sent to everyone who lives in the area and has registered for the service, alerting them to the description of the abductor.

In the future, the technology will make use of cell identification – triangulation using the signals exchanged between active mobiles and the nearest network base stations. This will allow texts to be sent en masse to everyone in a certain area at a certain time. We've already seen this sort of technology in use, in Hong Kong in 2003, where the local government sent unprompted texts to people within a kilometre radius of SARS outbreaks, warning them to be vigilant.

Paul Kent sees this as a way of rebuilding community. He says that: 'Everyone always tells us that community spirit is gone or is going, but as soon as there's a major incident, people come together. When they do, the networks just aren't in place to get information to people quickly enough. This is a way for people to constantly communicate with each other, to bring back their community spirit and make communities work better.'

More detailed studies of the impacts of ICT on social activity seem to lend support to this vision of ICT enhancing social interaction and community. The US research project, Syntopia, conducted by James Katz and Ronald Rice from Rutgers University, analysed the social behaviour of users and non-users of the Internet between 1995 and 2000. The research identified a clear trend: long-term use of the Internet was associated with more, not less, frequent socializing, as well as the same or a higher level of political and civil society involvement. Internet users were more likely to go out and see friends, although the study found that they spent more time away from their local community and generally knew fewer of their neighbours.[23] Syntopia's findings are backed by research carried out by the PEW Institute's Internet and American Life Project, which concluded that the use of email enhanced users' contact with family and friends and that email users generally had a richer social life.[24]

Data from France tells a similar story. A study conducted by Gilles Duranton and Sylvie Charlot of workplace communication practice produced similar results. The study analysed the relationship between use of email, use of telephones and face-to-face contact. It found that, although telephone contact tended to lead to increased face-to-face interaction, and vice versa, the role of email was somewhat different. Exchange of email didn't directly lead to more face-to-face contact, but did increase telephone usage. Importantly, the study also suggested that use of email wasn't replacing face-to-face or telephone communication.[25]

Keith Hampton of the Massachusetts Institute of Technology (MIT) led a study specifically into the use of ICT in a community context. He spent two years living in Netville (a pseudonym), a suburb of Toronto, observing the activity of other residents to try and find out whether online activity can supplement offline contact and help revive communities. Netville is like most suburbs in North America except that 61 out of the 109 homes are fitted with high bandwidth Internet connections (10Mbps). The research found that: 'The local computer network was used by residents as a means to exchange introductions, organize barbecues and parties, search for missing pets [etc]... Rather than isolating people in their homes, CMC [computer mediated communication] encourages visiting, surveillance, neighbour recognition and the maintenance of local social ties.'[26]

The evidence from online communities indicates that ICT can be used effectively to build trust and bolster social capital, but this works best when it is used to augment what is already there. The success of community websites, email lists and text services relies on them being connected to people's needs and integrated with other online and offline initiatives. In this way, electronic networks become additional channels for sharing relevant information between members of the community and providing social support.

We find something similar when we look at home based telework. ICT can keep remote workers in touch, but virtual contact alone is not enough to build trust.

Corporate social capital

The garage in Palo Alto where Bill Hewlett and Dave Packard started what has become one the world's largest information technology companies has been visited by politicians from around the world, looking for clues about what makes a company successful in the digital society. One of the reasons behind HP's success was its understanding of the value of trust to an organization. Dave Packard's time at General Electric had taught him that. There was a strict policy at General Electric that prevented employees from taking equipment home with them, even if they wanted to carry on working into the night. This stifled innovation and meant that equipment simply went missing rather than being borrowed and returned. Hewlett and Packard took the opposite approach, creating an atmosphere of trust, where workers were free to use equipment in their own time. This bred loyalty towards the company and a culture of innovation.

Many of the most successful ideas in the workplace are not the result of individual brainwaves, but the outcome of sharing knowledge and ideas informally over coffee or an after work drink. Equally, knowledge sharing ensures teams function effectively and tasks are completed on time. For knowledge to flow freely in an organization there have to be high levels of trust between individuals. As management experts Nahapiet and Goshal argue: 'no matter how knowledgeable employees are, if they believe they are working in a hostile low trust environment they will hoard information, avoid collaboration, and display very low levels of creativity'.[27]

In a book about corporate social capital, management consultants Don Cohen and Laurence Prusak described the daily interactions that build corporate culture and trust between individuals. They observed that: 'Co-workers define and redefine who they are as a group in part by sharing and monitoring reactions to events at work, news of the outside world, weather, the behaviour of bosses and subordinates, and the thousands of other subjects that form the currency of daily communication.'[28] The trust that allows knowledge to flow through a company is built through hundreds of everyday, seemingly insignificant encounters between colleagues.

In 'Sustainable development in the digital society', we saw that telework can benefit local communities by making it possible for people working at home to get more involved in local activities. At the same time, it poses a challenge to maintaining high levels of social capital within a company by reducing the amount of face-to-face contact between co-workers. This is particularly significant because telework is not an isolated phenomenon in the modern work place. It's the extreme end of a wider process of change in the way we work that's leading to greater mobility and flexibility of location.

Companies have tried to use technology to get round the problem of less face-to-face contact. Web conferencing or video conferencing, for example, allow interaction between employees in diverse locations. But the technology doesn't provide the rich social interaction of face-to-face encounters. As part of a survey on telework for Digital Europe, we interviewed a teleworker about a new web conferencing system his company had recently introduced. He was pleased with its basic performance, but said that it wasn't the same as a face-to-face meeting: 'In a face-to-face meeting there's the informal contact you have when you go into the room and the chat you have with everyone afterwards. You have the chance to pick up more information and maybe even get involved in opportunities as a result of that. When you have a web conference you're purely focused on the product update or whatever it might be. It's not the time or place for discussing other issues.' But it's the small talk that's most important for building trust between individuals and exchanging valuable information.

You come up against the same limitations with elearning. Teleworkers recognize that they can miss out on learning opportunities because so much learning takes place informally in the office. 'You learn less when you telework. When I used to work in an office environment I could go and talk to an expert whenever I wanted, or I would bump into an expert in the corridor, have a chat and learn something new. I'd also learn from other people in the office on a day-to-day basis. For example, if you're in a meeting every day you learn about chairing meetings. You definitely benefit from having different people in one room at the same time. You learn from being exposed to different views.'[29]

Elearning can be excellent for acquiring hard skills like IT, budgeting and technical skills. But it's not as good for picking up soft skills like emotional intelligence, communication and networking skills. Soft skills are learnt through the same social interaction that builds trust. Virtual communication as a form of social interaction is limited, both as a learning medium and as a way of building trust, especially if it's the only form of communication.

Building trust in the workplace is vital to the flow of knowledge within companies, but corporate social capital is also important for wider society. As the significance of extended family and local community has waned, the importance of the workplace for social interaction has grown. The American professor Norman Nie wrote that: 'The workplace has actually been elevated to one of the few remaining predictable sources of personal contact, collegiality and community in an increasingly isolated society, a place where people make friends, frequently find mates, and almost always share gossip and news'.[30] A seminar on work and social capital at Harvard University, led by Robert Putnam, concluded that: 'Two decades ago we began to recognize that our private lives affect our professional lives. Now we must recognize that the structure of modern work profoundly shapes our communities. People cannot compartmentalize their private, professional and civic lives. The job related decisions that employees and employers make have serious consequences for society as a whole.'[31]

There are benefits to remote working: it can give individual workers greater flexibility to balance work and family commitments. ICT creates new opportunities for this, but there are limitations to virtual communication when it comes to building corporate social capital that echo the limitations of purely online communities. Successful teleworking depends on companies allowing employees to find a comfortable balance between working at home or on the move and working in the office alongside colleagues. In box 5.2 Richard Reeves writes about the importance of companies matching technological innovation with organizational changes of this kind if they are to benefit fully from investment in ICT.

Trust in action

A telecoms expert from Poland we interviewed for Digital Europe reflected on why access to telephones had been restricted during the Communist era: 'The last thing the communists wanted in Poland was for people to communicate, that was dangerous for them. Restricting access to telephones was a form of social control, just as giving access to people now is a form of social liberation. The first thing that happened during martial law in the 1980s was that the telephones were all switched off.'[35] Trust between individuals is built through communication within social networks. By creating additional channels for communication, ICT can help build trust in the digital society.

Trust is critical to well functioning societies and economies. As we've seen, it's a kind of proxy measure of success, with all sorts of direct and indirect benefits. Building trust should be a priority for sustainable development. It's important on its own, but it's also important in the context of the other features of the digital society that we have looked at so far. Electronic networks are connecting us up on a global scale, creating feedback mechanisms that allow us to see the impacts of our actions beyond our immediate horizons. If

Box 5.2 *The workplace revolution that hasn't happened*
Richard Reeves

Recent advances in technology offer radical possibilities for better work. Sadly, they remain largely unfulfilled. Too many organizations are using technology to 'pave the dirt track', to do somewhat more efficiently the things they have always done, rather than to do something new.

Investments in whizzy IT systems without accompanying culture change carry significant financial and human costs. An MIT study of the effect of computers on productivity in 400 large US companies found a zero result: bad news for the IT industry! On closer inspection the firms broke down into two distinct categories. Those that introduced computerized systems alongside opportunities for employees to get involved – self-managing teams, devolved decision making – ended up with a sharp rise in output per head. But the ones that simply stuck computers on desktops, with no change in organizational structure, were, on average, *less* productive than firms that hadn't installed computers at all. It would have been better for these firms to have made a bonfire of their money in the company car park.

More importantly, the cultural lag in contemporary workplaces means that the socially liberating potential of ICT is being lost. Indeed, for many workers technology feels enslaving: laptops, the Internet and mobile phones have the potential to become the electronic tags of the modern employee. Joanne Ciulla, author of *The Working Life*, warns that information technology 'potentially makes us 24-hours-a-day, 365-days-a-year employees' – and that is how it feels to many people.[32]

But the majority of people, according to a poll for the iSociety project at The Work Foundation, believe that technology has the potential to allow them to work more flexibly.[33] And adverts for laptops and mobiles constantly stress the freedom they offer. Compare the ratio of ads showing people on beaches or in the bath with those more realistically showing people sitting on overcrowded commuter trains.

ICT blurs both sides of the line between work and life. It allows you to work outside the 'workplace' and it allows you to engage discreetly in non-work activities at your desk. (Employees sometimes have 'boss' keys that switch their screen view from eBay or Hotmail to a pre-arranged page of proper work.) Smart firms don't fret about this: they simply judge people on whether they are getting their work done.

Industrial work processes required people to be in the same place at the same time. It was a struggle, in the early industrial revolution, to get workers to accept this radical reduction in their autonomy – what I have else-where dubbed 'time sovereignty'. Hence the need for factory hooters and clocking-on machines. Historian Lewis Mumford said the true machine of the industrial revolution was not the steam engine, but the clock.[34] But eventually we got used to it. Organizations built on this conception of indus-trial time are struggling to come to terms with the post-industrial structure of time and space facilitated in large part by ICT. The continued existence of the rush hour is perhaps the most telling sign of how far we need to go.

There is an analogy here with the introduction of electricity. When it was first introduced into factories, electricity simply replaced the old steam-driven power sources for machines. Work remained organized in clusters around these machines, as was the norm in the steam age. For decades after the widespread adoption of electricity, factory layouts and systems remained essentially unchanged. It took a while for the realization to sink in that electricity ran along wires for no additional cost, and for the production line to be born.

We are in a similar transitional phase. Most workplaces have adopted ICT. Few have adopted new working patterns, cultures and performance systems to match. There are hopeful signs, here and there, of progress. But overall the fossilized cultures of most of our organizations are proving resilient to the challenges presented by technology. Right now, ICT is the workplace revolution that hasn't happened.

we use ICT as a pull rather than a push medium for information, people can be empowered to participate in feedback loops, rather than being lost in the noise.

But they still need to distinguish between information and misinformation. The third feature of the digital society – trust – allows us to navigate informa-tion, share and use the information we receive from others.

These three features begin to make the net work for sustainable develop-ment. The Welsh Assembly Government is putting them into practice in its attempt to build a sustainable future for Wales.

The Welsh Assembly Government, founded in 1999, aims to 'take social, economic and environmental issues into account in everything we do'.[36] It also has an ambitious strategy to promote the uptake and use of ICT and aims explicitly to use its ICT strategy to deliver on its commitment to sustainable development: 'We want a Wales that exploits ICT to deliver sustainable improvements in social and economic and health prosperity to achieve a better quality of life for all its citizens.'

An integral part of its strategy has been to spend £100 million on rolling out high quality broadband Internet access to the public, private and voluntary sectors throughout Wales and support this with capacity building. In June 2003, 47 per cent of schools and libraries and 85 per cent of doctors' surgeries in Wales had broadband access.

Wales recognizes that just putting the technology in place on its own is not going to motivate enough people to use it, and that relevant information is necessary as a trigger for widespread use. It also recognizes that the responsibility for making Wales more sustainable has to be a collective one: everyone needs to be involved.

The Assembly Government believes that the type of information on the network could be the key to satisfying both of these goals. It hopes that information about things that people care about – local recycling schemes, conservation groups, community centres, fresh food and so on – will bring people online and at the same time allow them to make changes in their own lives that will aid sustainable development.

It also hopes that providing people with meaningful information will build trust with the people of Wales and, over time, public participation will increase. According to Andrew Davies, the Minister for Economic Development and Transport: 'Many governments have understood that ICT can only be a tool for sustainable development if it is approached from the balance of the three Cs: accessible, affordable connectivity, useful, dynamic content and capacity building to develop skills throughout communities. In Wales we have understood that the essential extra ingredient is trust: built by working together in partnership at all levels and giving and receiving honest feedback.'[37]

Individually, none of the features of the digital society equips us adequately to meet the challenge of sustainable development. Connectivity alone can exacerbate social exclusion. Information alone can lead to confusion and erosion of trusted norms. We need trust to unleash the power of connectivity and information combined. That's why the strategy in Wales, bringing these three features together, creates an opportunity for progress towards a more sustainable future.

In the next chapter, we'll look at how virtualization – the shift from physical to virtual products and services delivered over the Internet – creates an opportunity to reduce the environmental impacts of consumer behaviour. Now that we understand how the features of the digital society can work for sustainable development, can we use them to realize the opportunities of virtualization?

VIRTUALLY SUSTAINABLE

In 2000 Kia, the Korean car manufacturer, launched its 'Think before you drive' advertising campaign in the UK. The campaign encouraged drivers not to use their cars for short journeys, only for long distance ones. Kia also gave away a mountain bike with every car sold in a certain range and organized 'walking buses', a network of parents to walk children to school instead of taking them by car. Kia recognized that improving the social and environmental impacts of its internal processes was important, but influencing consumers to behave more responsibly could have a greater effect. In 2002, each person in the EU consumed over €13,000 worth of goods and services and produced 535 kilograms of waste.[1] In the face of consumer stuff lust, it's becoming clear to businesses and governments alike that sustainable development needs as much emphasis on consumption as it does on production. In the digital society, as we move from physical to virtual products and services, sustainable consumption becomes a greater priority.

In the physical world, the material intensity of many products tends to be influenced most by the production phase. This explains why, historically, getting business engaged with sustainable development has focused on cleaning up production. With virtual products and services, consumers have far greater influence, because material intensity is no longer concentrated in the production and delivery phase of the product life cycle. Figure 6.1 shows how overall material intensity is distributed between producer, retailer and consumer when a CD is purchased in a music store (physical shopping), online (online shopping) and when a CD's worth of music is downloaded over the Internet (digital distribution). There's a marked downward shift in the distribution of material intensity across the value chain, making consumers as much the guardians of the environmental potential of virtual products as producers.

A more sustainable future depends on everyone taking responsibility for the impacts of their own behaviour. ICT provides a way of giving consumers the information they need to make choices in the interests of sustainable development. Getting this information out depends on producers using the network to

Figure 6.1 *The distribution of responsibility between producer, retailer and consumer in three different scenarios (share of total material intensity)*
Source: Wuppertal Institute

collect and communicate information about the impacts of their products to steer consumer behaviour in a more responsible direction. An open approach on the part of producers can build trust with consumers and encourage them to pull down the information they need. But, as the examples of digital music and ebanking will show, this mechanism alone is not enough to produce positive outcomes for sustainable development. It needs to operate in the right context to have that effect. This means government and business setting framework conditions that promote positive outcomes from responsible consumer behaviour. And that means developing the right policies and processes.

We chose digital music (a virtual product) and ebanking (a virtual service) as high profile examples of virtualization used by a relatively large number of people. We hoped that this research would allow us to draw conclusions that would be relevant to other products and services. To help with the research, Digital Europe partnered with the music company EMI and the UK high street bank, Barclays.[2]

Measuring the impact of virtual products

When 19-year-old student Shaun Fanning wrote a piece of code to help a friend download MP3 music files from the Internet, he had some big surprises in store. He could hardly have expected that a year later 67 million people worldwide would be using his invention, Napster, to get free access to music over the Internet, or that its popularity would prompt the Recording Industry Association of America to launch legal proceedings against him and eventually put an end to the Napster phenomenon. But what must have surprised Fanning most of all, was the stir Napster caused in environmental circles. Some even dubbed him an 'accidental environmental entrepreneur'.[3]

What were environmentalists so excited about? At the height of Napster's popularity in summer 2000, millions of users were sharing music over the Internet without a single physical product changing hands. Environmentalists saw two opportunities for resource savings: one in the dematerialization of products themselves – CDs in the case of Napster; the other in eliminating the transport and infrastructure needed to get products from manufacturer to consumer. If other products and services could be delivered virtually too, then there was real potential to improve the resource productivity of the economy as a whole.

After the initial excitement came a flood of early research suggesting that the impacts of virtualization were more complicated than environmentalists had first thought. Didn't the Internet have environmental impacts of its own? What happened if digital music files were burnt on to a CD rather than being stored on a computer hard drive? What would the overall impact be if the ease of downloading music meant that overall consumption went up? We set out to answer some of these questions in order to identify the real environmental potential – and the limits – of virtualization.

To begin to with, we needed a way of understanding what virtual transactions actually involve. They can be divided into three distinct phases:

1 The communications phase, in which buyer and seller exchange information and negotiate the sale, for example searching the Internet for a particular CD.
2 The production and delivery phase, in which the product is made and transferred to the buyer, whether by road, rail or Internet.
3 The payment phase, in which money changes hands between buyer and seller.

As Figure 6.2 shows, each phase can take place online or offline, creating a range of possible permutations. We can take virtualization to mean all three phases being online (option 7). It's worth remembering, though, that for the most part, ecommerce involves buying and selling physical products online that can't be made virtual. A virtual banana won't satisfy your hunger and a virtual haircut won't improve your image. With physical products, overall material intensity can only be marginally influenced by ICT (options 1–3), because the greatest impact tends to be in the production phase, which remains offline.

The Wuppertal Institute calculated the material intensity in different scenarios using the same methodology (MIPS) that we described in 'Infoworld'.

	Communication	Production & delivery	Payment
Option 1	online	offline	offline
Option 2	online	offline	online
Option 3	offline	offline	online
Option 4	offline	online	offline
Option 5	offline	online	online
Option 6	online	online	offline
Option 7	online	online	online

Figure 6.2 *Possible offline and online combinations for the three phases of an ecommerce transaction*
Source: Wuppertal Institute

For music, they looked at physical shopping, online shopping and digital download. In the physical shopping scenario, the customer buys a CD from a music store. In the online shopping scenario, the customer buys a CD over the Internet and in the digital download scenario the customer downloads 56 minutes of music (the length of the average CD) over the Internet. They followed the same comparative approach for ebanking, comparing the material intensity of paying a bill at a bank branch with that of paying the same bill online.

Lighter than air?

What happens to the environmental impact of music when the whole transaction moves from offline to online? (option 7 in Figure 6.2). The Wuppertal Institute calculated that downloading 56 minutes of music is twice as resource efficient as buying a CD online and more than two and a half times as resource efficient than going to a shop to buy a CD.

The savings come from every stage of the transaction. To start with, digital files replace physical CDs. The resources needed to make a physical CD give it an ecological backpack seven times its actual weight (see box 6.1). What's

---

Box 6.1 *The ecological backpack*

According to the MIPS methodology, to identify how much stuff a product or service uses, you need to measure the amount of material that's moved throughout the product's life span, including production, delivery, use and disposal. A good way of illustrating the result is to say that all this material (that doesn't end up in the final product) goes into an invisible 'ecological backpack'. The results can be surprising: the 'ecological backpack' of a 10g wedding ring is more than 5 tonnes.

Source: Wuppertal Institute

---

more, delivering music via the Internet eliminates the transport and infrastructure needed to get a CD from the factory to the consumer. In the case of EMI in Europe, CDs are taken by road from the factory to national distribution centres and on to local distribution hubs. From there they make their way to the retailer, often via another depot. Finally, the consumer makes a journey to the retailer to make a purchase. All in all the average CD travels well over 1000 kilometres before it reaches the consumer. In this time, its environmental backpack has increased to as much as 15 times its weight.

Figure 6.3 shows which phases in each of the physical shopping and digital download scenarios contribute most to the CD's overall material intensity.

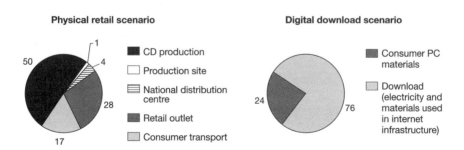

Figure 6.3 *Material impact of buying a CD in a shop and by digital download (per cent of total material impact)*
Source: Wuppertal Institute

The ebanking study produced similar results. Paying a bill online is two and a quarter times more resource efficient than paying the same bill at a branch. It's easy to see where some of the savings come from when we look at what goes on behind the scenes.

The data on the payment slip is entered into the bank's electronic system and transferred to a clearinghouse for payment. The slip itself also needs to be transported to the clearinghouse and stored. In the case of Barclays, slips are collected from a national network of 200 branches and transported to a single clearinghouse. Branches are often located close together, so slips can be collected from several branches in one trip. But even if one driver collects from 15 branches at once, because Barclays only has one clearinghouse in the country, the average round trip is still 500 kilometres. The calculation for branch banking also included the journeys made by individual consumers to their local branch, and the entire physical infrastructure associated with high street banking, such as clearinghouses and local branches. Figure 6.4 illustrates the most resource intensive phases in each scenario.

It's important to remember that both digital music and ebanking have material impacts and this goes for all virtual products and services. Even if all three phases of the transaction take place online, they remain rooted in the

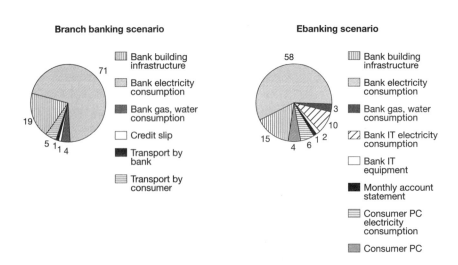

Figure 6.4 *Material impact of paying a bill at a branch and online (per cent of total material impact)*
Source: Wuppertal Institute

physical world to some extent, primarily because of the electricity consumed by the network infrastructure that makes virtualization possible. We'd do well not to neglect well-established environmental strategies such as switching to renewable energy to reduce the impact of electricity consumption.

The consumer rules

If the results for music and banking hold true in general, virtualization represents a real opportunity to reduce the environmental impact of products and services. But consumer behaviour could entirely change the picture, wiping out any environmental savings or even going the other way, making virtual products less resource efficient than their physical equivalents. The Wuppertal Institute identified a number of aspects of consumer behaviour that could influence the overall material intensity of virtual products and services:

- How quickly people upgrade Internet access devices such as PCs and handheld computers;
- The type of Internet connection people have (whether it's fast or slow);
- Whether the ease of buying online means people buy more;
- Whether consumers rematerialize virtual products and services, for example burning digital music on to CDs;
- Whether people buy online instead of or as well as buying on the high street.

Let's look at each of these in a little more detail.

Most of the material impacts of virtual products and services come from the electricity used by the technology needed to deliver them. According to the Wuppertal Institute's calculations, the consumer's computer and Internet connection account for a fifth of this. This is based on the assumption that the average consumer PC has a life span of four years. If the rate at which consumers upgrade their technology continues to increase, the average life span of the PC will decrease, and the overall material intensity of virtual products and services will rise. On current form, this seems likely. In the USA, 40 million computers became obsolete in 2001 alone.[4] In the UK, the average mobile phone is replaced after only eighteen months, although it has a life span of up to seven years.[5] And as electronic devices continue to get smaller, consumers are more likely to view them as disposable products and throw them away.

The speed with which consumers connect to the Internet has a strong influence over the material intensity of virtual products and services, simply because it affects the amount of time spent online. Figure 6.5 shows the amount of time it takes to download 56 MB of data with different connection

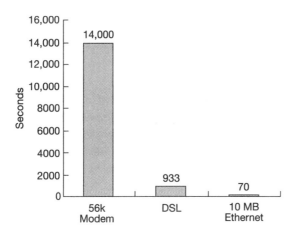

Figure 6.5 *Time taken to download 56 MB (average length album in compressed format) with three different connection speeds (seconds)*
Source: Wuppertal Institute

speeds (56 minutes of music – the average length of an album – in compressed format takes up around 56 MB). Downloading 56 MB takes four hours with a standard 56k modem but just over a minute with a 10 MB connection. And with every minute spent online waiting for the file to download, electricity is being used, making a 10MB connection in theory considerably more resource efficient than a 56k modem.

Faster download speeds don't always benefit the environment – it depends on how they're used. A fast Internet connection can encourage consumers to buy more online, because it's more convenient, wiping out the environmental savings made from buying virtual rather than physical products. This kind of rebound effect would lead to an increase in the overall environmental impact of consumption. Furthermore, because high-speed access to the Internet isn't charged by the minute, people tend to leave their computers on and connected to the Internet, pushing electricity usage up.

Environmental savings from virtualization can also be lost if consumers choose to rematerialize virtual products, for example by printing out emails or burning digital music files on to CDs. Virtual products are relatively new and as a result we tend to want to consume them in the same way as their physical equivalents, rather than adapting to the virtual environment. This has a significant effect on their impacts. The Wuppertal Institute calculated the ecological backpack of 56 minutes' worth of music when a consumer downloads it and then burns it on to a CD. If a blank CD is used, the ecological backpack more than doubles and only a minor resource saving is made compared to a CD bought in a music store.

Even where virtual products and services remain virtual, people are unlikely to completely abandon the old way of doing things. The majority of ebanking customers tend to use all the channels available to them – the Internet, the telephone and the local branch – rather than using ebanking exclusively. Digital downloads exist alongside CDs, ebooks have not closed down book shops and retailers offer online shopping as well as high street shopping. This means that the material intensity of virtual products can't be seen in isolation. Virtual products and services need to be considered as part of the full range of what's available to consumers if we're to get a full picture of the material intensity of consumption in the digital society.

Consumer behaviour has a major part to play in realizing the environmental potential of virtual products and services. We can enable people to act more in line with the goals of sustainable development by making the most of the network's capacity to disseminate information and empower them to use it effectively.

The net in action

When Apple added CD burners to their line of iMacs in 2001, they chose the slogan, 'Rip, Mix, Burn' for the marketing campaign. It's shorthand for the process of collecting the best tracks from several different albums and transferring them on to a CD using a computer. Apple could have taken a leaf out of Kia's book and used its marketing campaign to encourage consumers to adapt to the virtual environment and keep virtual products virtual, thereby benefiting the environment. But the company went the other way, encouraging consumers to rematerialize virtual products, and inadvertently promoted consumer behaviour that would reduce the environmental potential of virtualization.

The Internet gives people the opportunity to use information to take responsibility for their environmental and social impacts as consumers. One of the first suggested sustainability benefits of greater access to information on the Internet was as a boon to ethical consumerism. As James Wilsdon wrote in *Digital Futures: Living in a Dotcom World*: 'Traditionally, the barriers to ethical consumerism have been the difficulty of accessing products and the limited availability of reliable information. The Internet can overcome both of these problems.'[6] Any development of ethical ecommerce needs to consider ways of minimizing possible negative impacts. If a click of a mouse buys you something from Los Angeles or from London irrespective of which side of the

Atlantic you're on, greater take up of ecommerce could simply encourage air-freight and erode local economies.

The information is there for consumers who are interested in purchasing ethically, and there are examples where access to environmental information has changed consumer behaviour. The A–G energy efficiency grades introduced for household appliances in the UK have driven the least energy efficient appliances out of the market because consumers stopped buying them.[7] In the US, consumers saved enough energy to power 10 million homes in 2002 by purchasing computer equipment labelled with an Energy Star – a kite mark of energy efficiency (www.energystar.gov). It's unlikely that consumers were driven solely by environmental criteria when making these decisions, but access to environmental information allowed them to take environmental performance into consideration as part of a wider decision.

Unfortunately, ethical consumers are relatively thin on the ground. Although 30 per cent of consumers in the UK claim to take environmental, social and ethical criteria into consideration in making purchasing decisions, in reality the market share of ethical products rarely exceeds 3 per cent.[8] In fact, according to the Ethical Purchasing Index, the total value of the ethical wallet including banking and investments in the UK in 2001 was a mere 1.7 per cent of total sales in the key sectors tested – food, housing and lighting.[9]

This is where producers come in. Producers can use the network to provide consumers with information that will steer their behaviour towards more responsible consumption. This doesn't mean that products need to be explicitly labelled green or ethical. In fact, according to Mike Longhurst of advertising giant McCann-Erikson, that could be the wrong approach entirely: 'As soon as you tell people that product x is good for the environment, they'll assume it costs more and it won't work'.[10]

In the context of virtualization, producers could encourage consumers away from rematerializing digital content by building a simple question such as 'do you really want to print this again?' into the technology. This gives consumers the opportunity to make a positive environmental choice. However, in general, producers use their marketing muscle to influence consumer attitudes and beliefs against sustainable development goals, whilst their commitments to sustainable development (as far as they go) sit with another part of the company. Consumers get conflicting messages and this erodes trust in the information they receive.

Even the right kind of information flowing through the network won't lead to more responsible behaviour, unless the wider context in which it operates supports sustainable development. If we want to realize the environmental potential of virtualization, then government and business need to put in place framework conditions aligned to sustainable development.

Producer responsibility

Producers can encourage more responsible consumer behaviour through information and communication. But they can also influence consumer behaviour further upstream – in the design of products. To begin with, producers need to get better at designing products to fit consumer needs and habits rather than expecting consumers to accommodate technology. For example, Xerox and others are developing epaper, a promising technology that will allow consumers to read digital content as if it was on paper, with the added environmental advantage that the content can be changed and the paper reused. Another example is the Tablet PC. It allows users to make notes and scribbles on documents by writing on the screen with a pen, mimicking the way people make notes on paper.

Efforts should also be made to reduce the environmental impact of access devices. The trend towards miniaturization might suggest that this was happening anyway, with small devices using less material. But Digital Europe research found that miniaturization is not a long-term environmental solution. Working with HP, the Wuppertal Institute compared the material intensity of information processing using a laptop computer and a handheld computer. The laptop computer weighed 15 times as much as the handheld, but the manufacturing process only used around 7 times as much material. While in absolute terms the handheld used fewer resources, relatively it was more than twice as resource intensive than the laptop, indicating that there are diminishing returns from miniaturization.[11]

This means that we need to look elsewhere. In Europe legislation is pushing companies to improve the environmental efficiency of their products. For example, the Waste Electrical and Electronic Equipment Directive, which comes into force across the EU in 2004, makes producers responsible for the disposal of their products and sets targets for recycling and reuse. The Directive should reduce the environmental impacts of electronic waste but it will fall short of reducing the impacts of the materials used in production.

The use of recycled materials could substantially reduce the environmental impact of access devices. Primary copper, for example, a major raw material used in handheld devices, has a material intensity of 500 kg per kg, whereas secondary copper has a material intensity of only 9.7 kg per kg. The Wuppertal Institute recalculated the material intensity of producing both handheld and laptop computers, substituting 80 per cent recycled copper, aluminium and magnesium for primary materials.[12] Figure 6.6 shows the dramatic drop in material intensity that resulted.

Improving the eco-efficiency of each device will only get us so far if consumers continue to dispose of their electronic equipment long before its

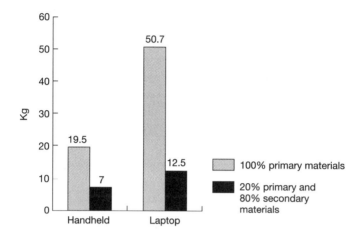

Figure 6.6 *Comparison of primary (non-recycled) and secondary (recycled) inputs for the casing and non-electronic components of a handheld computer and a laptop computer (kilograms)*
Source: Wuppertal Institute

use-by date. This calls for some lateral thinking. Responding to consumer demand doesn't have to mean selling a new product each time. Product upgrades could be delivered via software, consumers could rent products and exchange them for newer models rather than owning them outright and colleagues could share computing devices rather than each owning one and using it only occasionally. These are all examples of how producers can move away from a product focus to a service-based model that could be more environmentally efficient.

   Successful examples of new service-based models are hard to come by because the barriers to service innovation are high. For most companies, success is measured in terms of how much product they shift, not in terms of their success at managing long-term, service-based relationships. And, as consumers, we still get comfort from owning things. Nevertheless, the ICT sector is well placed to take a lead in service innovation. Already companies like HP have adopted this approach for their B2B clients, offering managed print services rather than a new printer, insuring consistent recycling of printer cartridges. In his contribution in box 6.2, Peter James of the UK CEED explores the contribution of ICT in facilitating product to service shift in other sectors – otherwise known as 'smart services'.

The challenge for companies is to make the shift from products to services work in consumer markets where status is often linked to ownership. Innovating new services to replace physical products won't be enough: producers need to inform and communicate with consumers to build acceptance of an economy focused on service-based delivery. Achieving this could result in less of a conflict between the sustainability policies that companies adopt and the way they market products and services. Widespread uptake of service innovation by consumers can work both in the economic interests of producers and in the interests of sustainable development.

Box 6.2 *Smart services*
Peter James

'Smart' stands for: sustainable, management-oriented, analytic, real-time and tracking.

Services are 'analytical' through the control achieved by identifying patterns and connections within large bodies of data. They are 'real-time' because much of the data being used is immediate in nature. And the 'tracking' typically relies on large numbers of small digital devices to monitor the position and state of key components in the system.

The use of smart services can make business both more productive and more sustainable. This is possible because of the increased processing power of ever-smaller ICT devices enabling precise measurements to be made quickly and action taken instantly.

Research by Green Alliance and SustainIT has highlighted how smart services are being developed in the UK and has identified a number of options for encouraging their introduction. We looked at the uptake of smart services in three sectors: agriculture, energy and transport.[13]

To be sustainable smart services need to create significant environmental and social benefit. In the case of agriculture, farmers have been able to reduce their use of nitrogenous fertilizer by up to 34 per cent by using GPS, accurate field mapping and data-gathering techniques to apply chemicals only where they are needed. Moreover, there have been fuel savings from reduced spraying of crops and the reduced use of unprofitable areas of land.

Fuel saving has been a major benefit of the deployment of smart services in energy and transport. Sophisticated thermometers taking regular readings have allowed more detailed information about energy consumption in buildings to be gathered. The analysis of the data quickly identifies wastage, such as heating controls set too high or equipment left on overnight, and provides accurate data on carbon dioxide emissions. In the case of transport, only 70 per cent of lorry movements in the UK involve the transport of freight. The remaining 30 per cent is effectively wastage through lorries returning to base empty. Smart services employing text messaging on mobiles to relay information to base are showing environmental benefits by rerouting vehicles away from congested areas, or instructing them to pick up new loads.

These examples are all 'management oriented' because they show clear business benefits and provide data that is practical and relevant. Smart services are synergistic with general business trends such as providing a greater role for suppliers and moving to intelligent, high-value-added activities. This means they're likely to happen anyway but, where progress is slow, a little policy support could be enough to tip the balance in their favour and encourage more widespread use.

But there are barriers to wider adoption. On mainland Europe, take up of smart services in agriculture has been slow, mainly because farms tend to be smaller and therefore have less capacity to invest in the ICT. One obvious solution would be for agrochemical and fertilizer suppliers to provide a service package including smart services rather than selling chemicals only.

In the case of energy, there's a danger that smart services are seen as intrusive and a technocratic approach to environmental improvement.

Finally, trends in business towards more rigorous reporting of social and environmental issues are likely to contribute to the development and uptake of smart services, as they allow better tracking of impacts. Mandatory corporate sustainability reporting could also be an important driver in the development and adoption of smart services.

Technological innovations such as the virtualization of products and services will continue to create new environmental and social opportunities. But realizing their full potential depends on how well we use the network to provide individuals with information that informs the choices they make and changes their behaviour. Doing this within a framework that promotes sustainable development could see progress towards virtuous use of virtual products.

So far in this book we've been broadly positive about the potential for sustainable development in the digital society. This may puzzle people whose everyday experience of ICT is quite different: mobiles ringing non-stop, unanswered emails filling inboxes and so on. Many people's perception is that modern technology is speeding up society unsustainably.

But the speed at which information flows across the network could be the final feature, alongside networks, information and trust, that makes the net work for sustainable development. Will speed send the system spinning out of control, or can we harness it in the long-term interests of our planet?

FASTER IS DIFFERENT

In 1965, Gordon Moore, co-founder of computer giant Intel, observed that the number of components on computer chips, and hence computer processing power, had doubled every 18 months for the previous five years. He predicted that this would continue into the future. Nearly 40 years later, his theory – now immortalized as Moore's law – holds true, and is expected to do so for the next ten years at least. The more processing power a computer has, the faster it works.

Data transfer rates have rocketed too. In the spring of 2003, 6.7 gigabytes of data, equivalent to two DVDs, were sent nearly 11,000 kilometres from the US to the Netherlands in less than a minute – a record-breaking speed of 923 megabits per second. That's 16,482 times faster than a normal dial up connection to the Internet. By the time you read this, the record will almost certainly have been broken, probably more than once.

Most of us are all too aware of the effects of speed in our everyday lives. 60 per cent of the adult population in the UK report that they suffer from stress, and more than half of these say that this has worsened over the last 12 months.[1] A quarter of British families only share a meal together once a month. With always-on communications keeping us permanently in touch, western society is moving more and more towards a 24/7 approach to life, enabling us to work more, do more and consume more. It's this 'Faster!' culture that leads us to take the taxi instead of walking, take the plane and not the train and eat the microwave meal. Even the term '24/7' is a new, quicker way of saying 'all day every day' or '24 hours a day, seven days a week'.

The question of how technology affects society has been around for a long time. In 1907 the French author Paul Adam was worried about the impact of the bicycle. The pedal bike allowed people to transport themselves four times faster than walking, and he was concerned that it would create a 'cult of speed' for a new generation.[2] There's a legitimate concern that the faster we live, the faster we consume the planet's finite resources and trash the natural system on which we depend. In this scenario, increasing speed is only driving us faster towards self-destruction. This is the fate that writer, Jay Griffiths, describes: '... the danger of speed is in its black opposite, in the instant of *expiring* – the stock market crash, the racing crash, the computer crash, the airline crash, a culture speeding up to its expiry date, the darkness over the event horizon, the moment of death.'[3]

Like Griffiths, Austrian philosopher Peter Heintel urges us to slow down, for our own sakes and for the sake of the planet. He's the man behind Tempus, the society for the deceleration of time. Every year, Tempus organizes a rather peculiar 100-metre race in the small town of Calw, near Stuttgart in Germany. The aim of the race is not to cover 100m in the shortest possible time, but to cover the distance in an hour. Slowness rather than speed, patience rather than power are required to win.

But do we have to slow down society if our goal is sustainable development? Is there no way to make the speed of technology work in our favour, instead of continually eroding our quality of life?

By connecting us, networks provide a mechanism for information to flow between individuals and trust ensures that the system works smoothly. Information is essential if we are going to change our behaviour in a way that promotes sustainable development. What happens if we add speed to the mix? Does the mechanism just spin out of control? As long as the mechanism is guided by the values of sustainable development, it could be possible to channel speed in the interests of our long-term sustainability. This is the way we can move our complex world towards a more sustainable future.

Unpredictable outcomes

In her seminal work *The Death and Life of Great American Cities*, urban theorist Jane Jacobs described how urban planners in the first half of the twentieth century wasted millions of dollars on failed regeneration initiatives. She pinpointed a fundamental flaw in the urban planning theories these initiatives were based on. Planners, contested Jacobs, had assumed that the structure of urban areas was scalable, that size was the only difference between the compact cities of old Europe and the massive, sprawling entities feasible in a country where the car was king and land was cheap. But bigger is not like smaller scaled up. Bigger is essentially different.

What is true for size is also true for speed. Faster is not like slower speeded up, faster is different, inherently different. Take cars as an example. Using a car has far greater implications than just being able to get from A to B in less time. It gives you the chance to travel further to shop, work and socialize. In the course of the twentieth century, being able to travel faster and further changed the structure of our settlements and the structure of our relationships and had a devastating effect on the environment.

Or take mobile phones. The technology allows more efficient use of time: you can let someone know if you're going to be late for a meeting so they can get on with something else in the meantime. If you're kept waiting you can use the time to make calls and organize other meetings. But, in no time at all, you feel compelled to make use of the dead time and with that comes extra pressure, impatience and the loss of time for thought and reflection.

The reason that some things are different when they're scaled up or made to go faster is that, like cities, societies and human beings, they are complex systems. One of the features of complex systems is their unpredictability. This stems from two fundamental characteristics. Firstly, they are underpinned by a network pattern: in network terms, they consist of an incredible number of nodes, and each node has an incredible number of connections to other nodes. Secondly, nothing in the system is fixed: the pattern of connections between nodes, and the amount, frequency and type of information flowing on these connections, can all change.

The unpredictability increases when different complex systems are put together. Try standing outside and throwing a ball in exactly the same way twice: it's almost impossible. Where the ball ends up is affected by, among other things, the conditions inside your body at the time and the weather conditions. Both of these are complex systems that modern science doesn't fully understand. Even if it did, we still wouldn't be able to predict where the ball would land. You, or the weather, do not determine what happens, it's a feature of the interaction between the two. The outcome is what is referred to as an 'emergent' property of a complex system.

In a complex environment, understanding how the different parts work doesn't necessarily tell you what will happen when you put them together. This was the point that Jane Jacobs was getting at when she criticized urban planners in America. Scaling up a small city creates an entirely different kind of city rather than the same city on a bigger scale because scaling up changes the interactions within the system. This makes complex systems highly unpredictable, but creates exciting possibilities for change. Changes in the system that appear insignificant can have dramatic system-wide effects. As the writer Malcolm Gladwell puts it: 'We need to prepare ourselves for the possibility that sometimes big changes follow from small events and that sometimes these changes happen very quickly'.[4]

In the digital society with social relationships increasingly mediated through electronic networks, the scale and speed at which human social networks operate is also increasing. This adds to the complexity of the system and means greater unpredictability as well as greater opportunities for change.

We've argued that global feedback mechanisms create the possibility for empathy to operate beyond small communities and that this is vital for meeting the challenge of sustainable development. The speed of the technology could make the system work more efficiently by increasing the rate at which information moves through the network, speeding up feedback. But ICT doesn't only create a mechanism for the negative feedback that keeps the system balanced. The network also supports self-reinforcing, positive feedback loops. Positive feedback loops were observed long before the term was coined. They are the 'vicious circles' and 'self fulfilling prophecies' of common parlance. It's positive feedback that keeps us on a path of ever-greater consumption, pollution and waste. If technology speeds up positive feedback, it simply fuels our unsustainable lifestyles. The critical question is whether we can channel speed in a way that increases the efficiency of negative feedback loops.

The speed of feedback

In August 1999, an earthquake measuring 7.4 on the Richter scale hit northwestern Turkey, killing as many as 14,000 people. Despite the destruction, the mobile network continued to operate, although at reduced capacity. The network infrastructure company Ericsson was on the scene within a day, bolstering the network against system overload. Ilter Terzioglu, the man responsible for Ericsson's base-stations in Istanbul, reported on the speed of Ericsson's response: 'Two days after the quake, half of the base-stations were in power in the disaster-zone. Many had been placed in containers on the roofs of houses now laying in ruins.' The rapid response to re-establish communication services meant that emergency workers could communicate with each other and call in extra help where it was needed. Action could be taken to save lives that might not otherwise have been possible.[5]

Information travelling quickly through the system doesn't just mean a quicker response in times of crisis. It can fundamentally alter our perception of the world and help us to connect apparently unrelated events. Take the gorillas in the Congo we mentioned earlier as an example. Being able to connect the high price of tantalum used in mobile phones and computer game consoles to the slaughter of Grauer's gorillas drew the attention of the world's press to the problem and stimulated a response from the electronics companies involved. There is now a strategy to develop regulated trade in tantalum from Central Africa. In a complex environment it becomes extremely difficult to make links between cause and consequence, especially where these are separated over time. With the increasing speed of technology, actions and their outcomes are more likely to be captured within the same timeframe, even on opposite sides of the world.

The speed with which information flows and the fact that so many people now have access to it makes the network difficult to control. This can work in the interests of greater transparency and accountability. In 1941 in London, thousands of people sheltered from the bombing by sleeping in underground railway stations. When a panic set in at Bethnal Green station there was a stampede for the exit and 173 people were killed. But the event wasn't reported until after 1945, as the British government of the day feared it would damage wartime morale.

Contrast this with events during the US-led invasion of Iraq in 2003. When a bomb exploded in a crowded marketplace in Baghdad on 28 March, killing over 60 people, both sides in the war blamed the other. The Iraqi authorities condemned US and British forces for targeting innocent civilians, while the USA and Britain suggested that it was most likely an Iraqi propaganda exercise to gain sympathy and support from opponents of the war around the world. The matter was taken out of government hands when Robert Fisk, Middle East correspondent with the *Independent* newspaper in the UK, reported finding fragments of the missile that destroyed the marketplace marked with the code MFR 96214 09. The western script suggested that it was an American missile and people flocked online to try to trace the code. Within a day, it had been linked to an armaments manufacturer in the USA. There's still uncertainty as to the authenticity of the link: was the fragment placed from somewhere else to create a story? But the speed with which people could access information made it trickier for the US authorities to evade difficult questions about their military strategy.

It's not just governments that can be forced to accept responsibility for their actions. The speed of feedback in the digital society may be more effective at holding companies to account. In 2001, activist Jonah Peretti decided to try the network out to see how quickly he could expose a company. At the time, Nike was running a promotion in which individuals could customize their trainers with a slogan of their choice. Peretti asked for his to be customized with the word 'sweatshop', but Nike refused. Peretti had saved his entire email correspondence with the company on his computer and promptly forwarded it to a few well-connected friends, knowing that they would pass it on. But even Peretti must have been surprised when it reached millions and he was receiving emails from strangers in Australia and New Zealand.

Jonah Peretti's email suggests that increasing the speed with which information flows between people could be a powerful driver for greater corporate responsibility. Greenpeace's campaign against Shell's dumping of the Brent Spar oil platform in the North Atlantic in 1995 acted as a massive spur to the corporate responsibility movement. In the same way, it may only take a few companies to fall foul of the speed of feedback to trigger wider change in business.

The same speed of information that can hold governments and companies to account can also work against sustainable development. For example, the speed and reach of ICT has allowed terrorists to organize on a global scale, with a level of flexibility and a distributed command structure that makes it extremely difficult to shut down their activities. Faster feedback can threaten global stability in other ways, when its direction is positive rather than negative. Nowhere can we see this more clearly than in the global financial system.

On 5 February 1997 the Thai property company, Somprasong Land, failed to pay $3.1 million of interest on a Euro convertible debt. This single failure involving a relatively small sum naturally went unnoticed by the wider financial market. How was anyone to know that this was the spark that set off a chain reaction that eight months later resulted in the biggest fall on the Dow Jones index until then – 554.26 points?

This kind of chain reaction is an example of cascading failure. Systems theorist Albert-Laszlo Barabási explains how the failure of a large but far from dominant property development company shook the world's financial markets: 'If we view the economy as a highly interconnected network of companies and financial institutions, we can begin to make sense of these events. In such networks the failure of a node has little effect on the system's integrity. Occasionally, however, the breakdown of some well selected nodes sets off a cascade of failures that can shake the whole system.'[6] Cascading failure results from the speed at which positive feedback works its way through the system, each action reinforcing the previous one rather than bringing the system back into balance.

Box 7.1 *Cascading failure*

Cascading failure can happen to different kinds of system, from power networks to biological, ecological or financial systems. Barabási explains the concept like this:

'When a network acts as a transportation system, a local failure shifts loads or responsibilities to other nodes. If the extra load is negligible, it can be seamlessly absorbed by the rest of the system and the failure remains effectively unnoticed. If the extra load is too much for the neighbouring nodes to carry, they will either tip or again redistribute the load to their neighbours. Either way, we are faced with a cascading event, the magnitude and reach of which depends on the centrality and capacity of the nodes that have been removed in the first round.'

Source: Barabási, *Linked*, 2002

Concern that the speed of technology is fuelling our unsustainable lifestyles and eroding ecosystems is well founded. But our fate is not sealed. We can use the speed of technology to increase the rate at which information flows through the network and increase the efficiency of negative feedback. If people have the capacity to respond to faster feedback, then change can promote a more sustainable future. To make the system work in this way it's not enough to have all the four features – networks, information, trust and speed – in place. We need to set our course by aligning the system to the values of sustainable development.

Sustainable development in a complex world

On a ship, the captain makes small adjustments throughout the journey to keep the vessel on course. If the wind blows the boat too far one way, he steers it back on course. He plots his course at the beginning of the journey, knowing that this allows him to respond to changes as they happen and yet still get where he wants to go.

Think about a sustainable society as our destination and sustainable development the course we need to take to get there. Just like the captain of a ship, we need to monitor our progress as we go, responding to changes as they happen. The speed of feedback and the global reach of information flowing over social networks, partly mediated by ICT, give us the means to do this. With our destination always in mind, aligning the speed of feedback to the values of sustainable development can keep us on course, allowing us to increase the efficiency of negative feedback and limit the effects of positive feedback.

Take cascading failure as an example of how this could work in practice. Our only hope of preventing it disrupting the global financial system is to change the context in which the system operates, not to try to control individual transactions and predict their outcomes. About 90 per cent of currency trading is speculative and absurdly short term. It's this rapid exchange of money across the globe that's at the root of the system's instability. Economist James Tobin has proposed a tax on cross-border currency transactions as a way of discouraging short-term trading. Support for the 'Tobin Tax' has gathered momentum around the world, with supporters in the Brazilian, Canadian, Finnish, French, Indian and Swedish parliaments. Over 300 respected economists worldwide support it, as well as numerous NGOs. If the tax was enforced it could act as the dampening mechanism necessary to bridle the runaway financial market.

Leadership from government and business on sustainable development to put in place the necessary policies and frameworks is critical if the speed of technology is to work for a more sustainable future. For both, this demands a step back from short termism and a greater willingness and capacity to respond to feedback.

For government, it means breaking away from a target setting approach that responds to immediate challenges and looking to longer-term, more holistic goals. In a paper on the role of government in a complex society, Tom Bentley, director of the UK think tank Demos, described how targets undermine the sustainability of public services such as the health service: 'Pushing up hospital bed occupancy rates improves the efficiency of the current system but stretches its resources in ways which reduce the institutions' ability to respond to crises and shocks, such as flu epidemics, whether or not they are foreseeable.'[7]

Adapting to the speed of feedback requires radical change in government structures. Centralized hierarchy remains the dominant model with targets too often imposed from above. Giving government the capacity to move more quickly depends, above all, on greater willingness to decentralize control, allowing other parts of society to develop innovative ways of realizing shared goals.

If anything, short termism is worse in business. In a survey of fund managers conducted by Watson Wyatt, 52 per cent described long-term return on investment as five years, and 24 per cent three years.[8] Soon after retiring as HP's chief executive, Lew Platt described the short-term culture of the business world he'd left behind: 'The world doesn't want you to slow down to make a good decision. Now you're lucky if you can sleep on it. Being considered as a slow decision maker is a terrible label to have.'[9] In this kind of environment, there's little room for the long-term responsibility inherent in sustainable development.

Companies have already begun to adapt to the speed of feedback by shifting towards more flexible, network structures. At present, these are set up to respond predominantly to feedback from the market. The challenge for business is to open up to other stakeholders and apply the same responsiveness and adaptability to its wider environmental and social impacts.

For individuals, it won't always be possible to slow down the pace of life in the way that Peter Heintel and the Tempus movement advocate. Nor is it realistic that people will always be able to disengage from the speed of the system. Take the workplace as an example. Swedish management experts, Ridderstråle and Nordström, highlight the growing pace of change in working life: 'Throughout most of the twentieth century, managers averaged one job and one career. Now, we are talking about two careers and seven jobs. The days of the long serving corporate man, safe and sound in the dusty recesses of the corporation, are long gone. Thirty years ago, we had to learn one new skill per year. Now, it is one new skill per day. Tomorrow it may be one new skill per hour.'[10]

Aligning the mechanism to sustainable development also crucially depends on giving individuals the capacity to respond to the increased speed of feedback. Otherwise, faster feedback will overwhelm us in much the same way as too much information can, rather than allow us to be more responsive. We need new skills to accommodate speed, such as the ability to handle and sort information and the ability to build and use networks. General competencies like these equip us to deal with change and take control of speed. They provide a foundation for learning new skills quickly in response to changing environments.

Sitting at a dinner with a group of complexity theorists, Kevin Kelly, co-founder of *Wired* magazine and member of the Long Now Foundation, raised the issue of long-term thinking. The scientists argued that, since complexity theory shows that even the near future is inherently unpredictable, it's futile to guess what future generations want and long-term planning will always be based on false predictions. In his response, Kelly pointed out the crucial difference between long-term planning and long-term responsibility: 'I agree that the former is futile, but that's no excuse to give up on the latter. The difference is between trying to control the future and trying to give it the tools to help itself. Believing in the future is not the same as believing that you can predict it or determine it.'[11]

Believing in the future means aligning the features of the new digital society to the values of sustainable development. In the final chapter of this book, we'll explore the values that underpin sustainable development and argue that the four features of the digital society create an environment in which these values could be powerful forces for change.

MAKING THE NET WORK

'Just as humans have always had some form of technology, so has that technology influenced the nature and direction of their development. The process cannot be stopped nor the relationship ended: it can only be understood and, hopefully, directed toward goals worthy of humankind.'[1]

At the start of this book, we were looking for signs that ICT would lead to a less resource intensive society, create new economic opportunities for regions in Europe's peripheries and reduce the environmental impact of the daily commute. There was little conclusive evidence one way or the other: ICT did not appear to be promoting a more sustainable society, nor did it appear to be detrimental to sustainable development. Yet when we look at the features of our digital society, we find ample evidence of change: ICT is changing the way we communicate, it's connecting us up to new people, creating global conversations and facilitating new mechanisms for feedback. It's giving us access to more information than we've ever had before and creating new channels to build trust in society. How can all this be happening without many clear signs of change at the economy-wide level?

It's no mystery really. Creating a world in which every individual can enjoy a decent quality of life without damaging the ecosystem we depend on is an enormous challenge and an urgent one. With no time to waste, we need to know whether or not we're heading in the right direction. That's why we've developed indicators to track our progress – carbon dioxide levels in the atmosphere, the level of pollutants in river water, the number of adults of working age employed, income inequality and so on. But the trouble with indicators is that we begin to think of sustainable development in these terms alone, rather than seeing them as useful guides. At its heart, sustainable development is a values driven concept. From time to time it helps to remind ourselves of the values that lie behind it.

In *Just Values*, Chris Tuppen and Jonathon Porritt put forward a set of generic values (regardless of cultural diversity, different norms and lifestyles) that would be conducive to a genuinely sustainable way of life:

- self-determination;
- diversity and tolerance;
- compassion for others;
- respect for the principle of equity;
- recognition of the rights and interests of non-humans;
- respect for the integrity of natural systems; and
- respect for the interests of future generations.

Few people would take exception to any one of these values and few people, if asked directly, would support gross inequality or environmental destruction. And yet both gross inequality and environmental destruction are endemic. How have we arrived at such a ludicrous situation? Why don't the actions of a company reflect the values of its employees or the actions of a government the beliefs of its people?

The problem is that people's individual values get lost in the system. We have seen that empathy is a driving force for sustainable development. Whereas individuals can cultivate it, organizations often can't, because the values of the individual members don't join up and so aren't expressed at a higher level.

Empathy – the ability to put ourselves in others' shoes – is what drives us to strive for tolerance, compassion, equity and so on. Without it, we perceive no injustice in the growing gap between rich and poor, no devastation in the loss of unique species, no crime in child poverty. Journalist Polly Toynbee powerfully sums up the social value of empathy in her recent book based on her experience of living in low wage Britain: 'Neither envy nor greed is as socially corrosive as lack of empathy, lack of sympathy with others, a pathological and deliberate refusal to put yourself in someone else's shoes and ask that essential question: would your society still look morally justified and fair if you were no longer looking down on it from the heights of ease, but up at it from the sluice room?'[2]

As well as the values behind sustainable development, it's important to build empathy into the system – empathy for others, both human and non-human, in this and future generations.

We saw in the last chapter how the risk of cascading failure is an inherent characteristic of the global financial system and that the Tobin Tax could be one way of preventing it, by changing the way the system works. Let's imagine we were building a social system from scratch and we wanted to build the values of sustainable development into it. What features would we design into the blueprint?

First, the system would be global. Sustainable development is a global challenge because all human beings depend on the same ecosystem: pollution doesn't recognize national borders, and everybody will feel the consequences of climate change. It's a shared challenge.

It would be an interconnected system in which all individuals would have equal opportunity to participate in a dense network of global connections. The openness and sharing of cultural heritage would promote diversity and foster tolerance.

The value of self-determination calls for individual empowerment. The system would encourage individuals to act independently rather than being controlled from the centre. This would allow it to draw on the richness of human diversity in tackling the challenge of sustainable development.

Compassion for others means that this interconnected, global system would need to have effective feedback mechanisms, to make us aware of the consequences of our actions and nurture the empathy that prompts us to change the way we behave. As a whole, the system would need the capacity to constantly change in response to feedback.

In recognition of the interests of future generations and the integrity of natural systems, the system would be guided by long-term responsibility towards human and non-human life. In short, a system designed to promote the values of sustainable development would have the following features:

- global reach;
- a dense network of interconnections between individuals;
- equal opportunities to participate;
- individual empowerment to act;
- effective feedback mechanisms to cultivate empathy;
- capacity for change in response to feedback; and
- long-term responsibility for human and non-human life.

These give us an alternative way of thinking about sustainable development. In this book, we've been looking at the four features of the digital society: networks, information, trust and speed. How do they measure up against the features we've just identified here? Do they get us any closer to a system that is built around the values of sustainable development?

The first feature we explored is networks. In the digital society, social relationships are increasingly mediated using ICT, primarily the Internet and mobile. This changes the quality of human social networks by facilitating a greater number of weak links into distant parts of the network that create a 'small world', enabling negative feedback on a global scale. Without feedback mechanisms, the system can't support the empathy that prompts us to respond and change. What is more, ICT could play a part in distributing valuable weak links more evenly across society, allowing more people to be active participants in the network.

The second feature of the digital society is the information that flows on the net. ICT gives us access to unprecedented amounts and for the first time puts it within easy reach. And, unlike broadcast media, ICT allows individuals to decide what information they want to receive and go in search of it. Relevant information could empower individuals to respond to feedback in the interests of sustainable development.

Trust is the third feature we discussed. It's our guide in the 'infoworld', allowing us to sort information from misinformation and take advantage of the network. In a low trust environment, we're slow to believe the information we receive and reluctant to share it with others. There are ways of building trust in information on the Internet and, used within existing social networks, ICT can create additional channels for building trust between people.

And finally speed, the fourth feature of the digital society. The speed of technology can erode people's quality of life but, at the same time, it could increase the efficiency of information through the network and the rate at which we receive and respond to feedback. If we can increase the rate of negative feedback, we could respond more quickly to environmental and social challenges and be more effective at holding people and organizations with authority to account.

Put the four features of the digital society together and what you end up with looks closer to a system built around the values of sustainable development than anything we've had before in the industrial age.

Perhaps we should have expected this. The Internet was created to be an open, global network in which everyone could participate on an equal basis. The founders of the Internet wrote their personal values into the software they pioneered, values that are remarkably similar to those of sustainable development. The global connections that we have identified as being so important for a sustainable future were equally the source of inspiration for Tim Berners-Lee, creator of the worldwide web. In his words: 'Hope in life comes from the interconnections among all the people in the world'.[4]

Before we get too carried away thinking that the net will inevitably work for sustainable development, we should remember that the features of a digital society could work in the opposite direction if the context in which they operate doesn't set sustainability as its goal.

In trying to achieve widespread access to ICT for all we could significantly increase resource use unless we actively seek to minimize the environmental impact of the network infrastructure. Shifting social relationships on to an electronic platform could simply reinforce – or even exacerbate – existing patterns of privilege unless we give everyone the skills to be active participants in the digital society.

The Internet gives us access to unprecedented amounts of information but this could overwhelm rather than empower us unless we can rely on trust to guide us. Virtualization could increase the environmental impact of products and services unless consumers can access trusted sources of information and take responsibility for their behaviour. The speed of technology could intensify already unsustainable lifestyles, fuelling consumption, eroding quality of life and threatening the planet's fragile ecosystems.

Unless we take into account the context in which ICT operates, there's a risk that technology will only reinforce the underlying structural problems in society. This makes it critical that technological change is accompanied by social innovation – change in our institutions, organizations and social arrangements – in line with the values of sustainable development. By itself, technological change is not a sufficient condition for a more sustainable future.

What does this mean in practical terms? What would the digital society look like if it fully took on the values of sustainable development? We can identify a range of criteria that should be satisfied for us to promote sustainable development in today's digital society.

At the highest level, we need to adopt an understanding of networks and sustainable development as organizing principles. The network is the pattern that underpins all forms of life and the relationships between them. It's only by understanding social and biological systems as highly interconnected networks that we can begin to make the world more sustainable. In theory, sustainable development has been a strategic priority in Europe since 2001, integrated across all policy areas and at the heart of all initiatives. In reality though, there are few examples of it being fully integrated at a strategic level. Until there is serious, consistent commitment to sustainable development, there is little hope of building a more sustainable future.

From these organizing principles flow a series of other criteria that need to be satisfied.

• Organizations recognize the importance of opening feedback loops and using the information they receive to align actions to goals.
• All people have the right to seek, receive and impart information regardless of frontiers.
• There is ubiquitous, affordable and inclusive access to ICT.
• Technology supports individual creativity and diversity.
• Access to the Internet isn't controlled by private interests but remains open to all as a shared public space.

- People are empowered to use technology for themselves rather than having solutions imposed on them. This means allowing individuals and communities to create ways of using ICT that suit their needs.
- Companies take responsibility for their direct impacts and make every effort to understand and improve these.
- Sustainable development sits at the heart of innovation and production (of products and business models alike).
- Companies invest in social capital among employees, along the value chain and in wider society, realizing its significance for their own sustainability.
- Organizations actively support a variety of different lifestyles and work patterns.
- People are equipped with the skills necessary for the digital society, such as the ability to build, contribute to and use social networks.
- Business and government use ICT effectively to improve the quality and relevance of the information they provide.
- Business and government are open to stakeholders and use ICT to involve them creatively in meeting their strategic goals.
- Consumers have access to social and environmental information and take responsibility for the effects of their behaviour.
- ICT is part of an integrated solution to sustainable regional development, alongside investment in infrastructure and the local knowledge base.

These criteria are based on a large number of recommendations made as part of Digital Europe. They're explored in detail in the three main Digital Europe reports, available to download from the project website.

Who's responsible for making sure we satisfy these criteria? As Martin Luther King put it: 'All of life is interrelated. We are all caught in an inescapable network of mutuality, tied to a single garment of destiny. Whatever affects one directly affects all indirectly.'[5] In the digital society, we are more aware of this than ever, and more empowered to use these interconnections to shape the future. An email from a primary school in North Carolina can reach 83 countries in a matter of days. One person searching on the Internet can hold the American military to account by linking the code on an exploded bomb to a missile factory in the USA. And an activist can use email to draw the world's attention to perceived wrongdoing by a global company.

In an interconnected system everyone is responsible: sustainable development must be a shared goal. Leadership from government and business is essential, but we also need these pivotal institutions to recognize how the net works for sustainable development and to use it to empower other parts of society, right down to the individual. This means exploiting the four features of the digital society that we've described: the network form, the information that flows on the network, the trust that makes that information valuable and the speed of feedback that gives it power. This is a system in which individuals matter. Just as people's values can scale up and be felt at a higher level, so the actions of individuals can also have system-wide effect. Small things can create big change in the digital society.

Humans are a technological species. As Fritjof Capra wrote: 'technology has crucially shaped successive epochs of civilization. We characterize the great periods of human civilization in terms of their technologies – from the stone age, bronze age and iron age, to the industrial age and the information age.'[6]

Each new wave of technological innovation has widened the scope of possibilities for human society. When humans were more intimately connected with natural systems, dependent on daylight, the seasons and physical strength, there was less choice about how to organize individual lives and society as a whole. Agricultural tools made it possible for people to live together in large numbers, leading to the rise of cities and a string of other profound social innovations. The invention of steam engines was the trigger for large-scale industry and radical changes in the economy. ICT in turn creates new possibilities of it's own.

A more technological society is not necessarily more removed from nature or set against it. It doesn't have to put the interests of the market before those of people. The digital society that we have described in this book is ultimately a society of greater choice. People have the power to make choices for themselves but, more importantly, we have more collective power to choose for society as a whole. How we use that power is up to us.

RECOMMENDED READING

If you'd like to explore some of the ideas we've covered in this book further, here's a list of other books you might find interesting.

Aldridge, S and Halpern, D (2002) *Social Capital: A Discussion Paper*, Performance and Innovation Unit, April 2002, available at http://www.cabinet-office.gov.uk/innovation/2001/futures/attachments/socialcapital.pdf

Barabási, A (2002) *Linked – The New Science of Networks*, Perseus Publishing, Cambridge, Massachusetts

Brown, J S and Duguid, P (2000) *The Social Life of Information*, Harvard Business School Press, Boston, Massachusetts

Buchanan, M (2003) *Small World: Uncovering Nature's Hidden Networks*, Orion, London

Capra, F (1997) *The Web of Life: A New Understanding of Living Systems*, Doubleday, New York

Castells, M (1996) *The Rise of the Network Society (The Information Age)*, Blackwell Publishing, Oxford

Castells, M (2001) *The Internet Galaxy: Reflections on the Internet, Business and Society*, Oxford University Press, Oxford

Chapman, J (2002) *System Failure: Why Government Must Learn to Think Differently*, Demos, London

Gleick, J (1999) *Faster: The Acceleration of Just About Everything*, Abacus, London

Hawken, P, Lovins, A and Lovins, L H (1999) *Natural Capitalism: Creating the Next Industrial Revolution*, Earthscan, London

Johnson, S (2001) *Emergence, The Connected Lives of Ants, Cities and Software*, Allen Lane, London

Lessig, L (2001) *The Future of Ideas: The Fate of the Commons in a Connected World*, Random House, New York

MacGillivray, A (2002) *What's Trust worth?*, New Economics Foundation, London

Miller, P (2002) *Open Policy: Threats and Opportunities in a Wired World*, Forum for the Future, London, available at http://www.forumforthefuture.org.uk/publications/

Porritt, J and Tuppen, C (2003) *Just Values: Beyond the Business Case for Sustainable Development*, British Telecommunications Plc and Forum for the Future, London, available on http://www.forumforthefuture.org.uk/publications/

Prusak, L, and Cohen, D (2001) *In Good Company: How Social Capital Makes Organizations Work*, Harvard Business School Press, Boston, Massachusetts

Putnam, R (ed.)(2002) *Democracies in Flux: The Evolution of Social Capital in Contemporary Society*, Oxford University Press, New York

Rheingold, H (2002) *Smart Mobs: The Next Social Revolution*, Perseus Publishing, Cambridge, Massachusetts

Romm, J (1999) *Cool Companies: How the Best Businesses Boost Profits and Productivity by Cutting Greenhouse Gas Emissions*, Earthscan, London

Watts, D (2003) *Six Degrees: The Science of a Connected Age*, WW Norton & Company, New York

Wilsdon, J (ed.) (2001) *Digital Futures: Living in a Dot-com World*, Earthscan, London

Zadek, S (2001) *The Civil Corporation: The New Economy of Corporate Citizenship*, Earthscan, London

ENDNOTES

Introduction

1 EITO, 2002
2 OECD, 2001
3 www.digital-eu.org

Sustainable Development In The Digital Society

 1 Negroponte, 1995
 2 Eurostat, 2003
 3 Pinelli et al, 2003
 4 James and Selwyn, 1998
 5 Evjemo et al, 2001
 6 Schallaböck et al, 2003
 7 Hopkinson et al, 2002
 8 Atkyns et al, 2002
 9 Hopkinson et al, 2002
10 Schallaböck et al, 2003
11 Leadbeater, 2002
12 Brown, 2001
13 Porritt, 2003
14 Weizsäcker et al, 1997
15 Kuhndt et al, 2003
16 ibid
17 MORI and Forum for the Future, 2002
18 CBI, 2002
19 Romm, 2002
20 Kuhndt et al, 2003
21 Ebusiness leaders were defined as companies that had average ebusiness use but were more likely to be using process applications such as eprocurement, production management and inventory management, and were more likely to use ebusiness in staff facilities, such as expenses, payroll and car sharing.
22 Goodman and Dawkins, 2003
23 Capra, 2002

24 Nordhaus, 2001
25 Coyle, 1996
26 Sheerin, 2002
27 Crafts, 2002; Nordhaus, 2002
28 Hill, 1999
29 Coyle and Quah, 2002; Coyle, 2003

Netting The Globe

 1 Capra, 2002
 2 Granovetter, 1973
 3 NUA, 2002
 4 ITU, 2002
 5 ibid
 6 Castells, 2000
 7 Barthel et al, 2000
 8 Romm, 1999
 9 Barthel et al, 2000
10 Hilty et al, 2003
11 Perri 6, 1997
12 Levy, 2002
13 Goodman, 2003a
14 Resnick, 2002; Mandag Morgen, 1999
15 Alakeson, 2003
16 Castells and Himanen, 2002
17 ibid
18 Porritt and Tuppen, 2003
19 Homer-Dixon, 2000
20 Capra, 1997

Infoworld

 1 Vitamin-e, event in London 2002 hosted by Forum for the Future, Demos and
    Ethical Media
 2 http://www.ohmynews.com/
 3 Gillmor, 2003
 4 Lessig, 2001
 5 Crystal, 2002
 6 Levine et al, 2000
 7 Henderson, 2001
 8 The term *hacker* refers to a skilled computer programmer, and not computer
    criminals.
 9 von Geibler et al, 2003
10 MORI and Forum for the Future, 2002
11 Available at http://www.globalreporting.org
12 Cowe and Porritt, 2002

13 Murray, 1998
14 Gleick, 2003
15 BBC News, 2000
16 Myerson, 2001
17 Crystal, 2002
18 Miller, 2002

Webs Of Trust

1 WEF, 2002
2 Ciancutti and Steding, 2000
3 WEF, 2002
4 O'Neill, 2002
5 Booz Allen Hamilton, 2002
6 Nielsen Net Ratings, October 2002
7 Department for Education and Skills, 2001
8 Sunstein, 2001
9 ACCA, 2003
10 MacGillivray, 2002
11 Putnam, 1995
12 Zak, 2003
13 ibid
14 Aldridge and Halpern, 2002
15 Shirky, 2002
16 Anbarasan, 2000
17 Resnick, 2000
18 Malone & Crowston, 1994
19 Resnick and Shah, 2002
20 Putnam, 2000
21 Resnick, 2001
22 http://www.communityalerts.co.uk
23 Katz and Rice, 2002
24 Castells, 2001
25 Charlot and Duranton, 2003
26 Hampton, 2002
27 Nahapiet and Goshal, 1998
28 Cohen and Prusak, 2001
29 Schallaböck et al, 2003
30 Nie, 1999
31 Better Together, 2000
32 Ciulla, 2000
33 iSociety and ICM, 2001
34 Mumford, 1934
35 Goodman, 2003a
36 WAG, 2000
37 Miller, 2003

Virtually Sustainable

1 Eurostat, 2003; EEA, 2001
2 Türk et al, 2003a; Türk et al, 2003b
3 Leadbeater and Willis, 2001
4 Goodman, 2003b
5 Fonebak and Shields Environmental, 2002
6 Wilsdon, 2001
7 Cowe and Porritt, 2002
8 Cowe and Williams, 2002
9 NEF and The Cooperative Bank, 2002
10 Wright, 2002
11 von Geibler, 2003
12 ibid
13 Hopkinson and James, 2002

Faster Is Different

1 MORI, 1999
2 Kern, 1983
3 Griffiths, 1999
4 Gladwell, 2000
5 Ericsson, 2000
6 Barabási, 2002
7 Bentley, 2002
8 Porritt and Tuppen, 2003
9 Meyer, 2001
10 Ridderstråle and Nordström, 2000
11 Brand, 1999

Making The Net Work

1 Kranzberg and Pursell in Capra, 2002
2 Toynbee, 2003
4 Berners-Lee, 1999
5 King, 1965
6 Capra, 2002

REFERENCES

ACCA (2003) *ACCA UK Award for Sustainability Reporting 2002: Report of the Judges*, The Association of Chartered and Certified Accountants, London

Alakeson, V (2003) *Inclusion in the Information Society: A Case Study with AOL Europe*, Forum for the Future for Digital Europe, available at http://www.digital-eu.org/publications

Alakeson, V; Aldrich, T; Goodman, J; Jorgensen, B and Miller, P (2003) *Project Theme Report: Social Responsibility in the Information Society*, Forum for the Future for Digital Europe, available at http://www.digital-eu.org/publications/

Aldridge, S and Halpern, D (2002), *Social Capital: A Discussion Paper*, Performance and Innovation Unit, April 2002, available at http://www.cabinet-office.gov.uk/innovation/2001/futures/attachments/socialcapital.pdf

Anbarasan, E (2000) 'Tim Berners-Lee: The Web's Brainchild', *UNESCO Courier*, September 2000, available at http://www.unesco.org/courier/2000_09/uk/dires.htm

Atkyns, R; Blazek, M and Roitz, J (2002) 'Measurement of Environmental Impacts of Telework Adoption Amidst Change in Complex Organizations: AT&T Survey Methodology and Results', *Resources, Conservation and Recycling*, vol. 36, 2002, pp267–285, Elsevier Science, USA

Barabasi, A (2002) *Linked – The New Science of Networks*, Perseus Publishing, Cambridge, Massachusetts

Barthel, C; Lechtenböhmer, G S and Thomas, S (2000) *International Climate Policy & the IT-Sector, Japan & Germany: 'Policy dialogue between Japan and Germany for facilitating co-ordinated measures to address global warming'*, Wuppertal Institute for Climate Environment Energy, Energy Division, Wuppertal, Germany

BBC News (2000) *Is E-mail Out of Ctrl?*, Thursday, 22 June, 2000, available at http://news.bbc.co.uk/1/hi/uk/801417.stm

Bentley, T (2002) 'Letting Go: Complexity, Individualism and the Left', *Renewal*, vol. 10, no 1, winter 2002

Berners-Lee, T (1999) *Weaving the Web: The Past, Present and Future of the World Wide Web by Its Inventor*, Texere Publishing, London

Better Together (2000), *Better Together: Report of the Saguaro Seminar on Civic Engagement in America*, John F. Kennedy School of Government, Harvard University, Cambridge, MA, available at http://www.bettertogether.org

Booz Allen Hamilton (2002) *International e-Economy Benchmarking: The World's Most Effective Policies for the e-Economy*, IAP/INSEAD, London

Brand, S (1999) *The Clock of the Long Now: Time and Responsibility*, Weidenfeld & Nicholson, London

Brown, L (2001) *Eco-Economy: Building a New Economy for the Environmental Age*, W W Norton & Co Inc, New York

Capra, F (1997) *The Web of Life: A New Understanding of Living Systems*, Doubleday, New York

Capra, F (2002) *The Hidden Connections: Integrating the Biological, Cognitive, and Social Dimensions of Life into a Science of Sustainability*, Doubleday, New York

Castells, M (2000) *End of Millennium (The Information Age vol. III)*, Blackwell Publishing, Oxford

Castells, M (2001) *The Internet Galaxy: Reflections on the Internet, Business and Society*, Oxford University Press, Oxford

Castells, M and Himanen, P (2002) *The Information Society and the Welfare State: The Finnish Model*, Oxford University Press, Oxford

CBI (2002) *Reality Bites: The Second Annual Report on e-Business in the UK*, CBI Publications, London

Charlot, S and Duranton, G (2003) *Communication Externalities in Cities*, INRA-ENESAD and London School of Economics, available at http://158.143.98.51/~duranton/Papers/ComCities.pdf

Ciancutti, M D and Steding T (2000) *Built on Trust: Gaining Competitive Advantage in Any Organization*, McGraw-Hill, New York

Ciulla, J (2001) *The Working Life*, Random House, London

Cohen, D and Prusak, L (2001) *In Good Company: How Social Capital Makes Organizations Work*, Harvard Business School Press, Boston, Massachusetts

Cowe, R and Porritt, J (2002) *Government's Business: Enabling Corporate Sustainability*, Forum for the Future, London

Cowe, R and Williams, S (2000) *Who are the Ethical Consumers?*, The Cooperative Bank, available at http://www.co-operativebank.co.uk/downloads/ethics/ethics_whoconsumers1.pdf

Coyle, D (1996) *The Weightless World: Strategies for Managing the Digital Economy*, Capstone Publishing Limited, UK

Coyle, D (2003) *Getting the Measure of Knowledge*, paper presented at the 3rd Social Study of IT Workshop, Department of Information Systems, London School of Economics, April 2003

Coyle, D and Quah, D (2002) *Getting the Measure of the New Economy*, The Work Foundation, London

Crafts, N (2002) *UK Real National Income 1950–98: Some Grounds for Optimism*, available at http://www.res.org.uk/society/pdfs/crafts.pdf,

Crystal, D (2002) *Interview: The Linguistic Wardrobe – Prof. David Crystal on Language and Technology*, Interview for Digital Europe, available at http://www.digital-eu.org

Datamonitor (2001) *eBanking Strategies in Europe 2002*, Datamonitor eFinancial Services report, October

Department of Education and Skills (2001) *Cybrarian Scoping Study*, London

EEA (2001) *Indicator Fact Sheet Signals 2001*, European Environment Agency, available at http://themes.eea.eu.int/Environmental_issues/waste/indicators/generation/w1_total_waste.pdf

EITO (2002) *European Information Technology Observatory 2002*, 10th edition, Frankfurt am Main, Germany

Ericsson (2000) *Ericsson Assists with Reconstruction in Turkey*, Ericsson response press room, January, available at http://www.ericsson.com/ericssonresponse/turkey_assists.html

EURO-OP (2003) *50 Years of Figures on Europe: 1952–2001*, Office for Official Publications of the European Communities, Luxembourg

Eurostat (2003) *Eurostat Yearbook 2003*, European Commission, Brussels

Evjemo, B; Yttri, B; Akselsen, A and Julsrud, T E (2001) *How does Telework influence on Quality of Life?: Findings Based Upon Interviews of Norwegian Teleworkers and their Close Social and Professional Networks*, R 41/2001, Telenor AS, available at http://www.telenor.no/fou/publisering/Rapp01/R41_2001.pdf

Fonebak and Shields Environmental (2002) *Fonebak Facts*, September 2002, available at http://www.shields-e.com/media/downloads.html

Gillmor, D (2003) *A New Brand of Journalism is Taking Root in South Korea*, Mercury News Technology Columnist, SiliconValley.com, May 18, 2003

Gladwell, M (2000) *The Tipping Point: How Little Things Can Make a Big Difference*, Little, Brown, New York

Gleick, J (1999) *Faster: The Acceleration of Just About Everything*, Abacus, London

Gleick, J (2003) 'Tangled Up in Spam', *The New York Times*, p42, February 9, 2003

Goodman, J (2003a) *Mobile Phones and Social Capital in Poland: A Case Study with Vodafone Group*, Forum for the Future for Digital Europe, available at http://www.digital-eu.org/publications

Goodman, J and Dawkins, J (2003) *Is eBusiness Good Business? Survey Key Findings*, Forum for the Future for Digital Europe, available at http://www.digital-eu.org/publications

Goodman, P S (2003b) 'China Serves As Dump Site For Computers: Unsafe Recycling Practice Grows Despite Import Ban', *Washington Post*, February 24, 2003, available at http://www.washingtonpost.com/ac2/wp-dyn?pagename=article&node=&contentId=A56653-2003Feb24&notFound=true

Granovetter, M (1973) 'The Strength of Weak Ties', *American Journal of Sociology*, issues 78, May, pp1360–1380

Griffiths, J (1999) *Pip Pip: A Sideways Look at Time*, Flamingo, London

Hampton, K (2002) *Netville: Urban Place and Cyberspace* (unpublished)

Henderson, D (2001) *Misguided Virtue: False Notions of Corporate Responsibility*, Institute of Economic Affairs, Hobart Paper 142, London

Hill, P (1999) 'Tangibles, Intangibles and Services: A New Taxonomy for the Classification of Output', *Canadian Journal of Economics*, vol. 32, issue 2, pp426–446

Hilty, L; Behrendt, S; Binswanger, M; Bruinink, A; Erdmann, L; Fröhlich, J; Köhler, A; Kuster, N; Som, C and Würtenberger, F (2003) *Der Einfluss moderner Gerätegenerationen der Informations- und ommunikationstechnik auf den Energieverbrauch in Deutschland bis zum Jahr 2010 – Möglichkeiten zur Erhöhung der Energieeffizienz und zur Energieeinsparung in diesen Bereichen*, (Final Report for the Federal Ministry for the Economy and Work), available at http://www.isi.fhg.de/e/publikation/iuk/Fraunhofer-IuK-Abschlussbericht.pdf

Homer-Dixon, T (2000) *The Ingenuity Gap: How Can We Solve the Problems of the Future*, Jonathan Cape, London

Hopkinson, P and James, P (2002) *Service Innovation for Sustainability: A New Option for UK Environmental Policy?*, Green Alliance, London, available at http://www.green-alliance.org.uk/Documents/Reports/service%20innovation%20for%20sustainability.pdf

Hopkinson, P; James, P and Maruyama, T (2002) *Teleworking at BT: The Economic, Environmental and Social Impacts of its Workabout Scheme, Report on Survey Results*, SusTel and Bradford University, Peterborough, available at http://www.sustel.org/outputs.htm

iSociety and ICM (2001) *iSociety Survey Data*, available at http://www.theworkfoundation.com/pdf/icmresdata.pdf

ITU (2002) *World Telecommunication Development Report 2002: Reinventing Telecoms*, International Telecommunications Union

Jacobs, J (2002) *The Death and Life of Great American Cities*, Random House, London

James, P and Selwyn, J (1998) 'The Pros & Cons of a Wired World', *Green Futures*, September/October 1998, pp24–27

Katz, J E and Rice, R E (2002) 'Project Syntopia: Social consequences of Internet Use', *IT & Society*, vol. 1, issue 1, summer 2002, pp166–179 available at http://www.itandsociety.org

Kern, S (1983) *The Culture of Time and Space: 1880–1918*, Weidenfeld & Nicolson, London

King, M L (1965) *The Reverend Dr. Martin Luther King, Jr. at Oberlin*, Commencement Address at Oberlin College, Ohio, June 1965, available at http://www.oberlin.edu/external/EOG/BlackHistoryMonth/MLK/MLKmainpage.html

Kuhndt, M; Geibler, J; Türk, V; Moll, S; Schallaböck, K O and Steger, S (2003) *Project Theme Report: Virtual Dematerialisation – eBusiness and Factor X*, Wuppertal Institute for Digital Europe, available at http://www.digital-eu.org/publications/

Leadbeater, C (2002) *Up the Down Escalator: Why the Global Pessimists are Wrong*, Viking, London

Leadbeater, C and Willis, R (2001) 'Mind Over Matter: Greening the New Economy', in Wilsdon J (ed.) *Digital Futures: Living in a Dot-com World*, Earthscan, London

Lessig, L (2001) *The Future of Ideas: The Fate of the Commons in a Connected World*, Random House, New York

Levine, Locke, Searls & Weinberger (2000) *The Cluetrain Manifesto: The End of Business as Usual*, Ft.com, Edinburgh

Levy, S (2002) 'Living in the Blog-osphere', *Newsweek*, August 2002, issue 26

MacGillivray, A (2002) *What's Trust Worth?*, New Economics Foundation, London

Maignan, C; Ottaviano, G; Pinelli, D and Rullani, F (2003) *Comparative Regional Case Study with Piedmont, Ruhr and Wales*, Fondazione Eni Enrico Mattei for Digital Europe, available at http://www.digital-eu.org/publications

Malone, T W and Crowston, K (1994) 'The Interdisciplinary Study of Coordination', *ACM Computing Services*, issue 26, pp87–119

Mandag Morgen (1999) *Kompetencerådets rapport 1999*, Huset Mandag Morgen, Copenhagen

Meyer, C (2001) 'The Second Generation of Speed', *Harvard Business Review*, April 2001

Meyerson, G (2001) *Heidegger, Habermas and the Mobile Phone*, Icon Books, Cambridge

Miller, P (2002) *Open Policy: Threats and Opportunities in a Wired World*, Forum for the Future, London

Miller, P (2003) *Cymru Ar-Lein and Sustainable Development: A Case Study with the Welsh Assembly Government*, Forum for the Future for Digital Europe, available at http://www.digital-eu.org/publications

MORI (1999) *Stress At Work Already Affects Almost 60% Of The Working Population – And The Problem's Getting Worse*, MORI, International Stress Management Association UK and Royal & Sun Alliance Healthcare & Assistance, available at http://www.mori.com/polls/1999/stress2.shtml

MORI and Forum for the Future (2002) *Forum for the Future: Research into Corporate Sustainability and Ebusiness*, MORI, unpublished

Mumford, L (1934) *Technica and Civilization*, Harcourt Brace Jovanavich Publishers, Orlando, Florida

Murray, B (1998) 'Data Smog: Newest Culprit in Brain Drain', *APA Monitor*, vol. 29, March 1998

Nahapiet, J and Goshal, S (1998) 'Social Capital, Intellectual Capital, and the Organisational Advantage', *Academy of Management Review*, issue 23:2, April 1998, pp242–266.

NEF and The Co-operative Bank (2002), *Ethical Purchasing Index 2002*, available at http://www.co-operativebank.co.uk/ethics/ethicalpolicy_consumerism.html

Negroponte, N (1995) 'Get a Life?' *Wired Magazine*, issue 3.09, September 1995, Wired, available at http://www.wired.com/wired/archive/3.09/negroponte.html

Nie, N (1999) 'Tracking our Techno Future: What are the Social Consequences of Innovation?', *American Demographics*, July 1999

Nielsen Net Rating (2002) *Online Banking Proves Popular*, Nielsen NetRating, November 2002

Nordhaus, W (2001) *The Progress of Computing*, Cowles Foundation Discussion Paper 1324, September 2001

Nordhaus, W (2002) *The Health of Nations: The Contribution of Improved Health to Living Standards*, RES lecture, NBER Working Paper 8818, March 2002

NUA (2002) *How Many Online?*, available at http://www.nua.ie/surveys/how_many_online

O'Neill, O (2002) *A Question of Trust: The BBC Reith Lectures 2002*, Cambridge University Press, Cambridge

OECD (2001) *Employment Outlook*, OECD

Perri 6 (1997) *Escaping Poverty: From Safety Nets to Networks of Opportunity*, Demos, London

Pinelli, D; Maignan, C and Bellini, E (2003) *Project Theme Report: Ebusiness and Sustainable Regional Development in Europe*, Fondazione Eni Enrico Mattei

Porritt, J (2003) *Sustainable Capitalism*, Forum for the Future, London, unpublished

Porritt, J and Tuppen, C (2003) *Just Values: Beyond the Business Case for Sustainable Development*, British Telecommunications Plc and Forum for the Future, London

Putnam, R (1995) 'Bowling Alone: America's Declining Social Capital', *Journal of Democracy*, January 1995

Putnam, R (2000) *Bowling Alone: The Collapse and Revival of American Community*, Simon and Schuster, New York

Resnick, P (2002) 'Beyond Bowling Together: SocioTechnical Capital', in Carroll, J M (ed.) *HCI in the New Millennium*, Boston, Addison-Wesley, chapter 29, pp647–672

Resnick, P and Shah, V (2002) *Photo Directories: A Tool for Organizing Sociability in Neighborhoods and Organizations*, available at http:\\www.si.umich.edu/~presnick/papers/whothat/

Ridderstråle, J and Nordstrøm, K (2000) *Funky Business*, ft.com, Edinburgh

Romm, J (1999) *Cool Companies: How the Best Businesses Boost Profits and Productivity by Cutting Greenhouse Gas Emissions*, Earthscan, London

Romm, J (2002) 'The Internet and the New Energy Economy', in Pamlin, D (ed.) (2002) *Sustainability at the Speed of Light*, WWF Sweden, Solna

Schallaböck, K O; Utzmann, I; Alakeson, V and Jorgensen, B (2003) *Telework and Sustainable Development: A Case Study with the Global e-Sustainability Initiative (GeSI)*, Wuppertal Institute and Forum for the Future for Digital Europe, available at http://www.digital-eu.org/publications

Shearman, C (2000) *Local Connections: Making the Net Work for People and Communities*, European Association of Community Networking, conference speech, available at http://communityconference.vicnet.net.au/99/papers/shearman1.pdf

Sheerin, C (2002) *UK Material Flow Accounting*, Economic Trends no. 583, June 2002, Office for National Statistics

Shirky, C (2002) *Communities, Audiences, and Scale*, April 6, 2002, available at http://shirky.com/writings/community_scale.html

Sunstein, C (2001) *Republic.com*, Princeton University, New Jersey, USA

Toynbee, P (2003) *Hard Work: Life in Low-pay Britain*, Bloomsbury, London

Türk, V; Kuhndt, M; Alakeson, V; and Ritthoff, M (2003b) *The Social and Environmental Impacts of Digital Music: A Case Study with EMI*, Wuppertal Institute and Forum for the Future for Digital Europe, available at http://www.digital-eu.org/publications

Türk, V; Kuhndt, M; Alakeson, V; Aldrich, T and von Geibler, J (2003a) *The Social and Environmental Impacts of eBanking: A Case Study with Barclays PLC*, Wuppertal Institute and Forum for the Future for Digital Europe, available at http://www.digital-eu.org/publications

Vitamin-e (2002) *Supporting Southern Voices Online*, events, available at http://www.vitamin-e.net

von Geibler, J; Ritthoff, M and Kuhndt, M (2003) *The Environmental Impacts of Mobile Computing: A Case Study with HP*, Wuppertal Institute for Digital Europe, available at http://www.digital-eu.org/publications

WAG (2000) *Learning to Live Differently*, Wales Assembly Government, Cardiff

WEF (2002) *Results of the Survey on Trust*, World Economic Forum, available at http://www.weforum.org/site/homepublic.nsf/Content/Annual+Meeting+2003%5CResults+of+the+Survey+on+Trust

Weizsäcker, E; Lovins, A and Lovins, H (1997) *Factor Four: Doubling Wealth, Halving Resource Use*, Earthscan, London

Wilsdon, J (2001) 'Dot-com Ethics: e-Business and Sustainability', in Wilsdon, J (ed.) (2001) *Digital Futures: Living in a Dot-com World*, Earthscan, London

Wright, M (2002) 'Sustainable Stufflust?', *Green Futures*, July/August 2002, p. pp22–26

Zak, P (2003) 'Trust', *Journal of Financial Transformation*, The Capco Institute, issue 7, 2003

ACRONYMS AND ABBREVIATIONS

ACCA	Association of Chartered and Certified Accountants
BBC	British Broadcasting Corporation
B2B	Business to business
CBI	Confederation of British Industry
CD	Compact disc
CMC	Computer mediated communication
CNN	Cable News Network
CSR	Corporate social responsibility
DSL	Digital subscriber line
EMPA	Swiss Federal Laboratories for Materials Testing and Research
EU	European Union
EU25	The 15 member states of the European Union and 10 candidate countries
FEEM	Fondazione Eni Enrico Mattei
GDP	Gross Domestic Product
GeSI	Global eSustainability Initiative
GPS	Global Positioning System
GRI	Global Reporting Initiative
GVA	Gross value added
HP	Hewlett Packard
ICT	Information and communications technology
ISP	Internet service provider
IT	Information technology
ITU	International Telecommunications Union
IZT	German Institute for Future Studies
Kg	Kilogram
MB	Megabyte
MIPS	Material input per service unit
MIT	Massachusetts Institute of Technology

NEF	New Economics Foundation
NGO	Non-governmental organization
OECD	Organization for Economic Cooperation and Development
PC	Personal computer
SARS	Severe Acute Respiratory Syndrome
TMR	Total material requirement
UK	United Kingdom
UKCEED	UK Centre for Economic and Environmental Development
UN	United Nations
US	United States
USA	United States of America
WAG	Welsh Assembly Government
WEF	World Economic Forum

INDEX

References to text boxes by contributors are printed in *italic*. References to illustrations are printed in **bold**.